W9-AUY-064

Social Issues in Literature

War in Tim O'Brien's
The Things They Carried

Other Books in the Social Issues in Literature Series:

Social Issues
in Literature

War in Tim O'Brien's
The Things They Carried

Gary Wiener, Book Editor

GREENHAVEN PRESS
A part of Gale, Cengage Learning

GALE
CENGAGE Learning

Detroit • New York • San Francisco • New Haven, Conn • Waterville, Maine • London

GALE
CENGAGE Learning

Christine Nasso, *Publisher*
Elizabeth Des Chenes, *Managing Editor*

© 2011 Greenhaven Press, a part of Gale, Cengage Learning

Gale and Greenhaven Press are registered trademarks used herein under license.

For more information, contact:
Greenhaven Press
27500 Drake Rd.
Farmington Hills, MI 48331-3535
Or you can visit our Internet site at gale.cengage.com

For product information and technology assistance, contact us at

Gale Customer Support, 1-800-877-4253
For permission to use material from this text or product, submit all requests online at www.cengage.com/permissions

Further permissions questions can be emailed to permissionrequest@cengage.com

Articles in Greenhaven Press anthologies are often edited for length to meet page requirements. In addition, original titles of these works are changed to clearly present the main thesis and to explicitly indicate the author's opinion. Every effort is made to ensure that Greenhaven Press accurately reflects the original intent of the authors. Every effort has been made to trace the owners of copyrighted material.

Cover illustration by Lewis O. Thompson. Used by permission.

LIBRARY OF CONGRESS CATALOGING-IN-PUBLICATION DATA

War in Tim O'Brien's The things they carried / Gary Wiener, book editor.
    p. cm. -- (Social issues in literature)
  Includes bibliographical references and index.
  ISBN 978-0-7377-5459-9 (hardcover) -- ISBN 978-0-7377-5460-5 (pbk.)
  1. O'Brien, Tim, 1946- Things they carried. 2. Vietnam War, 1961-1975--Literature and the war. 3. War in literature. I. Wiener, Gary.
  PS3565.B75T4893 2011
  813'.54--dc22

                                                                    2011005931

Printed in the United States of America
2 3 4 5 6   17 16 15 14 13

Contents

Chapter 3: Contemporary Perspectives on War

Introduction

For thousands of years, warriors were depicted as heroic demigods striding into battle, and writers often euphemized the horrific nature of war by covering it over with flowery language. "The real war will never get into the books," American poet Walt Whitman famously said of the Civil War (1861–65) in his memoir *Specimen Days*. He was only partly correct. When Whitman depicted "a heap of amputated feet, legs, arms, hands . . . a full load for a one-horse cart," outside a makeshift Civil War hospital, he himself began to put the real war into the books. Stephen Crane, E.E. Cummings, Erich Maria Remarque, Ernest Hemingway, Norman Mailer, and Joseph Heller, among others, followed Whitman's lead and began to use realistic descriptions of war in their fiction. Tim O'Brien's depictions of the Vietnam War (with combat occurring 1965–75) are cited as among the most searing and eloquent of such efforts. Belying Whitman's prediction that "Future years will never know the seething hell and the black infernal background of countless minor scenes," O'Brien delivers a graphic portrayal of such personal moments in his collection of related stories *The Things They Carried*.

One irony of O'Brien's success in this respect is that he has never tried to tell the truth about Vietnam. In portraying a war full of ambiguities, he treats what actually occurred on any given day as less important than a careful rewriting to reflect the soldier's experience, focusing on what he calls the story truth.

The Things They Carried is O'Brien's fourth book. The preceeding three also treat his Vietnam War experience. The first, *If I Die in a Combat Zone*, is a nonfiction memoir. His second book and first novel, *Northern Lights*, tells the story of two brothers—one who goes to war and one who does not—and their complex relationship after the wounded veteran returns home. The National Book Award–winning *Going After Cacciato*, O'Brien's third work, is a Vietnam War fantasy based on the bizarre premise of a soldier going AWOL (absent without leave) and walking from Vietnam to Paris; the novel focuses on what occurs when the character's fellow soldiers are sent to retrieve him. The complex narrative mixes gritty true-to-life depictions of war with fantastically impossible events that recall the literary genre of magical realism, in which the real and the supernatural are merged. The *New York Times* said, "To call *Going After Cacciato* a novel about war is like calling *Moby-Dick* a novel about whales." *The Things They Carried*, though ostensibly a war story, is also much more.

The novel puzzles many readers precisely because O'Brien tells the truth about war without giving a factual account of his wartime experiences. He does not sugarcoat the ugliness or euphemize the gruesome, but he blurs the truth between fact and fiction. His protagonist is named Tim O'Brien, but that character is not the Tim O'Brien who wrote the book; instead, he is a fictional persona created for the purpose of driving the story. The fictional O'Brien is a writer and has produced the same books as the author, but unlike the real O'Brien, the character has a daughter, and he returns to Vietnam to bury his closest friend's moccasins in the field that served as the village latrine. The real writer revisited Southeast Asia and the scene of his war service only in 1994, four years after *The Things They Carried* was published. A disclaimer at the beginning of the book informs readers that the characters and events are all imaginary, yet the work is "lovingly dedicated" to the fictional men of Alpha Company. O'Brien seems to suggest that life is as confusing as war.

In the title story the author works hard to establish a sense of verisimilitude, a term applied to literature that creates a likeness to life. O'Brien uses lists of the things that the soldiers carried to convey the reality of his tale. This focus on accuracy is heightened by O'Brien's tone. In a book-length study of the author, *Understanding Tim O'Brien*,[1] Steven Kaplan suggests, "More striking than this obsession with even the minutest detail . . . is the academic tone that at times makes the narrative sound like a government report." Using lists in literature is a practice as old as Homer's great war epic, *The Iliad*, and was popularized in American writing by Whitman. O'Brien applies the technique in a uniquely poetic fashion. The men's burdens range from their equipment (such as helmets, weapons, radios, and food) to their diseases (malaria, dysentery, and so on) to their emotional baggage (including fear, panic, shame). These long catalogs have the cumulative effect of displaying the awful encumbrance the soldiers bear in being responsible for an entire country's honor and world standing. O'Brien narrates their stories with such clarity and power that the reader cannot help but think of them as real, breathing human beings, though the disclaimer insists that they are fictitious.

Take the character of Lieutenant Cross, for example. Featured in the book's opening story, Jimmy Cross is drawn so realistically that the reader has no trouble believing in him. The realism is supported when Jimmy Cross visits the first-person narrator (later identified as "Tim O'Brien") years later and the two reminisce about the war. The effect is jarring. Given that there is a character with the same name as the author of the book, could there not be a real-life lieutenant? And yet O'Brien endows Jimmy Cross with mythological and quasi-religious significance that renders him a fictional creation. His name, for example, bears the same initials as Jesus Christ. Once the reader makes this connection, the significance of Jimmy's last name becomes eminently clear. In a story whose chief metaphor is weight, the things the soldiers *carried*, Jimmy Cross is accountable not only for himself but also for the lives of his men. He also bears responsibility for his country's success in its quest to defeat the demon communism in Southeast Asia. In a sense, he is carrying the entire

United States of America on his shoulders. It is no coincidence that his would-be girlfriend, Martha, has the same name as the matriarch of the country, Martha Washington. All of this symbolism suggests that the name Jimmy Cross is a complete fabrication and that, therefore, the character is too—or perhaps not.

Thus O'Brien puts the real war into the books by not telling the truth. It is a strange, paradoxical notion, but one that makes perfect sense, as much sense as the truism that we fight wars to achieve peace.

Another paradoxical way in which O'Brien tells the stark truth about war is by not talking about it, as if it were too overwhelming to put into words. In the opening story, company member Norman Bowker continually instructs his fellow soldier Kiowa to "shut up" every time the Native American attempts to recount the tale of their friend Ted Lavender's death. As O'Brien said in an interview in 2010, "All the guilt, the responsibility, the trauma. Silences are one of the main coping mechanisms." But the author also commented on the danger of silence: "It can be destructive if it eats at you and finds its way out in booze and drugs and violence."[2]

Like Hemingway, O'Brien often centers his stories on the aftermath of warfare, focusing on characters who suffer from some form of post-traumatic stress disorder. One enduring truth found in O'Brien's work is that while warfare may end, it is never truly over for the veteran. In *Northern Lights*, Harvey Perry returns from Vietnam with a "pretty souvenir," a wounded eye that has left him half blind. Though he will never talk about how he was injured, continually claiming that he does not remember, O'Brien constantly focuses his descriptive attention on that eye as the central feature of Harvey's face. Harvey's injury symbolizes his only partial ability to see his way back to normal society. He is still half-blinded to the ways of civilian life and lives in a state of perpetual longing after pipe-dreams, never fully able to settle back into a traditional role. Similarly, in the story "Speaking of Courage" from *The Things They Carried*, Norman Bowker returns from war aimless, spending his time driving his father's car repeatedly around the same lake, rehearsing what he would say if someone would just listen to what he had to tell about his war experiences. But Norman realizes that talking about the war is futile. During his eleventh circuit of the lake, he comes to this conclusion: "There was nothing to say. He could not talk about it and never would." Norman Bowker commits suicide three years after his return from Vietnam.

O'Brien knows the struggles veterans face with post-traumatic stress disorder. In a 1994 article, "The Vietnam in Me," he writes, "Last night suicide was on my mind. Not whether, but how. Tonight it will be on my mind again. Now it's 4 AM, June the 5th. The sleeping pills have not worked. I sit in my underwear at this unblinking fool of a computer and try to wrap words around a few horrid truths." Tim O'Brien the novelist attempts to tell the stories that his fellow veterans cannot, but he recognizes that what is left out can be as powerful as what is included. He realizes that some vets do not want the most embarrassing parts of their service revealed. When Lieutenant Jimmy Cross visits the fictional Tim O'Brien after the war is over, Cross asks the writer to "make me out to be a good guy, okay?" He then adds, "And do me a favor. Don't mention anything about—." O'Brien agrees to the request, saying, "No . . . I won't." The reader never learns what it is that Jimmy had asked O'Brien not to mention. Is it the death of Ted Lavender, which occurred on Cross's watch? Is it his crying jag after Lavender died? Or is it something altogether different, something that O'Brien actually did leave out of *The Things They Carried*? Whatever it is, O'Brien purposely omits this delicate information that so troubles the lieutenant even many years after the war. War—and war stories, O'Brien suggests—must be handled with care.

The Things They Carried has achieved such success that in 2010, on the twentieth anniversary of its publication, it was the subject of numerous celebratory events across the country. The book has been a selection in the National Endowment for the Arts' program The Big Read and has become required reading in many high schools and colleges. The viewpoints that follow examine O'Brien's work from a wide variety of perspectives. They cover O'Brien's life; explore the subject of war in his book, both as a whole and as individual stories; and present contemporary opinions on modern warfare from Vietnam to Afghanistan. These viewpoints dramatize the depth and power of O'Brien's narrative and suggest why this book has become a modern classic.

Notes

1. Steven Kaplan, *Understanding Tim O'Brien*. Columbia: University of South Carolina Press, 1995.
2. Catherine Roberts, "Carrying the Story," *Rochester (NY) Democrat and Chronicle*, October 24, 2010.

Chronology

1946

William Timothy O'Brien is born on October 1 to William T. O'Brien and Ava E. Schultz O'Brien in Austin, Minnesota.

1956

The O'Briens move to Worthington, Minnesota.

1964

O'Brien enters Macalaster College in St. Paul, Minnesota.

1968

O'Brien graduates from Macalaster with honors, having served as student body president during his senior year.

He is drafted into the US Army in August and begins his service.

1969–1970

O'Brien serves a thirteen-month tour of duty in Vietnam.

1970

O'Brien enters the graduate program in government at Harvard University.

1971–1972

O'Brien serves as an intern at the *Washington Post*.

1973–1974

O'Brien takes a leave of absence from Harvard to work as a national affairs reporter for the *Washington Post*.

1973

O'Brien publishes his Vietnam War memoir, *If I Die in a Combat Zone*.

He marries Ann Weller.

1974–1976

O'Brien returns to Harvard for further study, then leaves to pursue a full-time writing career.

1975

O'Brien's first novel, *Northern Lights,* is published.

1976

O'Brien receives an O. Henry Memorial Award for his short story "Night March."

1978

O'Brien's novel *Going After Cacciato* is published.

O'Brien's story "Speaking of Courage" wins an O. Henry Memorial Award.

1979

Going After Cacciato wins the National Book Award.

1985

O'Brien publishes the novel *The Nuclear Age.*

1990

The Things They Carried is published. The novel is a finalist for the Pulitzer Prize.

1991

The Things They Carried wins the Melcher Award.

1992

The Things They Carried wins the Prix du Meilleur Livre Étranger in France.

1994

O'Brien returns to Vietnam for the first time since the war.

He publishes his essay "The Vietnam in Me" in the *New York Times Magazine.*

His novel *In the Lake of the Woods* is published.

1995

In the Lake of the Woods wins the James Fenimore Cooper Prize for best novel based on a historical theme.

1998

O'Brien's novel *Tomcat in Love* is published.

1999

O'Brien begins teaching in the graduate creative writing program at Texas State University.

2002

O'Brien's novel *July, July* is published.

2009

O'Brien's essay "Telling Tales" is published in the *Atlantic Monthly.*

CHAPTER 1

Background on Tim O'Brien

The Life of Tim O'Brien

Vietnam War Reference Library

The following selection from the Vietnam War Reference Library traces the major events in Tim O'Brien's youth and young adulthood that led him to a successful career as a writer. O'Brien grew up in a small town in Minnesota and went to Macalester College, where he took part in antiwar activities. Having earned a scholarship to do graduate work at Harvard, he was dismayed to learn that he had been drafted by the US Army. Unable to summon the nerve to dodge the draft, O'Brien found himself serving in one of the more active and dangerous areas of Vietnam. After his discharge from the army, he returned to the United States and began to craft his war experiences into both nonfictional and fictional accounts. The publication of his novel Going After Cacciato, *which won the National Book Award, moved O'Brien to the forefront of modern American writing. His book* The Things They Carried *cemented his stature as a major figure among twentieth-century American novelists.*

Award-winning author Tim O'Brien is one of America's best-known writers about the Vietnam War. A Vietnam veteran, O'Brien has drawn upon his wartime experiences to write several classic literary works about the conflict, including *Going after Cacciato* (1978), *The Things They Carried* (1990), and *In the Lake of the Woods* (1994).

Growing Up in Minnesota

Tim O'Brien was born in the small town of Austin, Minnesota, on October 1, 1946. His parents were William T. O'Brien, an insurance salesman, and Ava (Schulz) O'Brien, a schoolteacher. Looking back on his childhood, O'Brien described himself as a shy and lonely youngster who had difficulty making friends. As he grew older, he used magic tricks as a way to gain approval and applause from his peers. "There's a real appeal in that for a lonely little kid in a lonely little town, to get that kind of love and applause and to feel you have some control," O'Brien recalled in *Booklist.*

After graduating from high school, O'Brien enrolled at Macalester College in St. Paul, Minnesota. He eventually became one of Macalester's leading student activists. In fact, he campaigned for a wide range of social and political causes around campus, ranging from efforts to reform the college's grading system and its policies toward women students to participation in demonstrations against the Vietnam War. . . .

O'Brien Receives His Draft Notice

In 1968 O'Brien graduated from Macalester with a bachelor's degree in political science. An honor student, he was offered a full scholarship to continue his education at Harvard University. But then he received his draft notice to report for duty in the U.S. Army. O'Brien spent the next several months agonizing about whether to obey the draft. He thought about going to jail or fleeing the country in order to avoid being sent to fight a war in which he did not believe. But he knew that many of his family and friends would be angry and ashamed of him if he did not answer his country's call. "It was the most terrible summer of my life," he told the *New York Times.* "My conscience kept telling me not to go, but my whole upbringing told me I had to."

O'Brien finally decided to obey his draft notice. But he later confessed in the *New York Times Magazine* that he did so only because "I could not bear the prospect of rejection . . . by my family, my country, my friends, my hometown. I would risk conscience and rectitude [moral righteousness] before risking the loss of love. . . . I was a coward. I went to Vietnam."

Author Tim O'Brien explores war in his novel The Things They Carried. © Jerry Bauer. Reproduced by permission.

O'Brien in Vietnam

O'Brien arrived in Vietnam in February 1969. He was assigned to an infantry unit in Quang Ngai Province, a region of central South Vietnam along the South China Sea. O'Brien soon learned that he had been sent to one of the country's deadliest places. Viet Cong guerrilla fighters [who fought for Communist North Vietnam] roamed throughout the forests and villages of the region, despite the best efforts of American infantry squads and airpower.

O'Brien spent the next several months taking part in patrols deep into the Quang Ngai countryside. His unit regularly passed through My Lai, a village where hundreds of unarmed peasants had been brutally massacred by U.S. troops only a few months earlier. The My Lai atrocity was concealed from the American public and U.S. soldiers for more than a year, but O'Brien recalled that the atmosphere surrounding the village was tense and hateful. "The My Lai area . . . scared . . . me, to be honest with you," he told *Booklist*. "It was a spooky, evil place on the earth. . . . It scared everybody, and that was before we knew what had gone on."

As the weeks passed by, O'Brien became accustomed to the death and destruction that surrounded him. "Back in 1969, the wreckage was all around us, so common it seemed part of the geography, as natural as any mountain or river," he wrote in the *New York Times Magazine*. "Wreckage was the rule. Brutality was S.O.P. [standard operating procedure]. Scalded children, pistol-whipped women, burning hooches [huts], free-fire zones [regions in which U.S. soldiers had approval to shoot anyone they saw], body counts, indiscriminate bombing and harassment, fire, villages in ash, M-60 machine guns hosing down dark green tree lines and any human life behind them."

Returning Home

In March 1970 O'Brien was discharged from the U.S. Army with the rank of sergeant. He returned home with a Purple Heart medal he received after suffering a minor shrapnel wound while out on patrol. Years later, O'Brien marveled at the swift change in environment that he and other soldiers experienced when they left the jungles of Vietnam to return to their hometowns. "It was fast and effortless, just like gliding out of a nightmare," he recalled in *Publishers Weekly*.

Upon returning to America, O'Brien enrolled at Harvard University to pursue a degree in government. But the year he spent in Vietnam continued to haunt him, and he began to compose a journal in which he described his wartime experiences. As O'Brien worked on the book, he spent hours thinking about the grim and horrible events that he witnessed during the war. But he also spent a lot of time reflecting about the ways in which Vietnam gave him a greater appreciation for love, friendship, and the simplest pleasures of life.

O'Brien's first book, *If I Die in a Combat Zone, Box Me Up and Ship Me Home*, was published in 1973. This nonfiction work described all stages of O'Brien's Vietnam experience— from military training through combat to homecoming—in a series of story-like essays that were praised for their realism and honesty. "In a style which is lucid, relaxed, razor-sharp, and consciously dispassionate, the wasteland of Vietnam unreels before us," wrote one reviewer in *The New Statesman*.

Writing About the War

O'Brien followed up *If I Die in a Combat Zone* with *Northern Lights* (1975), his first novel. The story follows two brothers whose lives become endangered during a stormy cross-country ski trip. One of the brothers is a Vietnam War veteran who is loved by his patriotic father, while the other is the family "failure" who did not fight for his country. As the ski trip turns into a perilous struggle, however, it is the "failure" who takes the lead in ensuring their survival.

Northern Lights received mixed reviews from critics, but the experience of writing a novel convinced O'Brien to dedicate himself to a literary career. "There came a point when I had to decide where I was going to devote my time," he told

Publishers Weekly, "and I decided that I wanted to be a writer and not a scholar." He dropped out of Harvard in 1976 and began writing full-time.

Going After Cacciato

In 1978 O'Brien published *Going after Cacciato*, a novel that wove two storylines together into one powerful work. Part of the novel describes the experiences of one battered, war-weary platoon of U.S. infantrymen as they struggle to survive in Vietnam.

The other section of the book follows the war-ravaged fantasies of one member of the unit. Assigned to night guard duty, the soldier imagines chasing an actual deserter from the platoon—Cacciato—all across Vietnam to the streets of Paris, France.

Going after Cacciato was widely hailed as one of the finest books ever written about the Vietnam War. It won the prestigious National Book Award and established O'Brien as one of the country's leading voices on the war. It also led many Vietnam veterans to contact him by telephone or letter to share their own wartime experiences. O'Brien confessed, however, that their letters and phone calls left him with mixed feelings. "It has been a bittersweet experience," he told the *Christian Science Monitor*. "The letters mean a lot because I had wanted to touch on something that was common to us all. But I found myself involved in so many hour-long phone calls from shattered guys that it was like reliving the war all over again."

The Things They Carried

In the mid-1980s O'Brien concentrated on writing projects that explored a variety of non-Vietnam topics. But in 1990 he returned to the Vietnam War again with a short story collection called *The Things They Carried*. Many of the events described in *The Things They Carried* closely mirrored O'Brien's own experiences. In addition, many of the interrelated stories are set in O'Brien's home state of Minnesota or in Quang Ngai Province, where he was stationed during the war. Moreover, the collection features several characters who are closely based on soldiers that O'Brien met in Vietnam. Finally, the volume is narrated by a character named "Tim O'Brien." Still, O'Brien has described the book as a work of fiction.

When *The Things They Carried* was published, it immediately attracted a great deal of popular and critical attention. *Booklist* hailed it as a "compassionate, complex, magnificent novel of self-acceptance and renewal." The *New York Times Book Review* offered a similar assessment, calling the collection "one of the finest books, fact or fiction, written about the Vietnam War. . . . By moving beyond the horror of the fighting to examine with sensitivity and insight the nature of courage and fear, by questioning the role that imagination plays in helping to form our memories and our own versions of truth, [O'Brien] placed *The Things They Carried* high up on the list of best fiction about *any* war." And *Publishers Weekly* commented that "O'Brien's meditations—on war and memory, on darkness and light—suffuse the entire work with a kind of poetic form, making for a highly original, fully realized novel. . . . The book is persuasive in its desperate hope that stories can save us."

The Things They Carried received several literary awards in the months following its publication, and it was nominated for a number of other prestigious honors. Since then, O'Brien's collection has retained a prominent place in discussions about enduring Vietnam War literature. In fact, *The Things They Carried* is now generally regarded as the single greatest work of literature ever written about the American experience in Vietnam.

Returning to Vietnam

O'Brien wrote about Vietnam once again in 1994's *In the Lake of the Woods*. This novel explores the disappearance of a woman after her husband's political career is destroyed by revelations that he was present at the My Lai massacre in Vietnam. *In the Lake of the Woods* received several honors, including recognition from the *New York Times Book Review* as the best book of fiction of 1994. But it did not enjoy the same level of critical or popular success as *The Things They Carried*.

O'Brien also made a special journey to Vietnam in 1994. He returned to Quang Ngai Province, the region where he had served during the war. During his trip, he met many men and women who had been caught up in the war, including former Viet Cong officers and survivors of the My Lai massacre. Upon returning to the United States, O'Brien said that the trip helped heal some of the lingering emotional wounds from his first Vietnam experience. "There was a new Vietnam in my thoughts," he told *Booklist*. "It's a nice feeling to find the geography, to walk in the backyard again and not really remember what happened so much as feel blown away by the utter peace that's replaced what was horror."

O'Brien continues to explore a variety of subjects in his writing. His 1998 novel *Tomcat in Love*, for example, centered on the relationships between men and women. But he remains best known for his works on the Vietnam War. Indeed, it is the power of O'Brien's Vietnam-related works that led the *San Francisco Examiner* to call him the "best American writer of his generation" in 1998.

Civilians Do Not Understand War

Tim O'Brien

Tim O'Brien is the award-winning author of The Things They Carried, Going After Cacciato, In the Lake of the Woods, *and other works.*

In this essay, author Tim O'Brien writes about his war experiences and how they affected his life. For O'Brien the Vietnam War was a blur, and he felt a continuing sense of unreality, especially with regard to the deaths he witnessed. The writer chafes at those who feel left out because they missed the war: He suggests that all they missed was a horrible experience and that those who fled to Canada to escape the war may have shown more bravery than those who fought. O'Brien is surprised by how little today's students understand about Vietnam. He believes that there are numerous parallels between Vietnam and the US response to the terrorist attacks of September 11, 2001. In both cases, he writes, we have wrongly demonized our enemy, and there can be no possibility of a productive resolution when we do so.

I've never thought of myself as a war writer. Ultimately I'm trying to speak to everybody about the heart under pressure, the incredible spiritual pressure of seeking the right thing to do under difficult circumstances. I don't write about maneuvers and bombing and how guns work. I don't explain the mechanics of ambushes and patrols. These things bore me. They bored me even in Vietnam. I was too overwhelmed by the feeling of doing something really wrong and evil to be interested in the military nuts and bolts of it all. I was also too terrified.

The Unreality of War

It was just a blur of going from village to village through paddies with no sense of destination, or mission, or purpose.
You'd just wake up and go to a village, search it, and leave.
Somebody might die or not, and you'd come back a month
later to the same damn village and do it again. It was like going in circles and not really achieving anything. You weren't
winning hearts and minds and you weren't winning ground.
You didn't know who to shoot unless they were shooting at
you. The enemy seemed to be everywhere and nowhere.

The fundamental experience was like being in Wonder-
land. The old anchors of reality were gone. I've just finished
something I've never written about before. A guy had been
shot, a dying American guy, and he kept mumbling the same
word over and over. Most often people would say stuff like
"Momma" or "Daddy." They'd go way back into primitive
childhood stuff. This guy kept saying the word *ever* over and
over. Why that word? Maybe I just didn't hear him right.
Maybe it was *never*. But it sounded like *ever* and he kept saying it over and over. Those are the kind of memories you're
never going to wholly understand. We knew very few answers
to anything in Vietnam, and thirty years later you find the
ambiguities waking you up in the middle of the night. You see
that guy's chest bubbling and blood coming out of his mouth
and hear that word *ever* just over and over.

War and Guilt

I was in Quang Ngai Province, out in the middle of this
bombed-out mess. The whole province was wasted. The My
Lai massacre [the murder of hundreds of unarmed peasants
in the village of My Lai by US troops] was just part of it. By
the time I got there in 1969 our bombing and artillery fire
had destroyed basically ninety percent of the dwellings. The
villages were sometimes almost deserted. There had been a
pacification program in which people had been moved out of

their hamlets into refugee camps. Many villages only had about twenty or thirty people still there, mostly old people and VC [Viet Cong, members of the North Vietnamese–supported Communist guerilla movement]. We were really hated. It was just so patent. You could see the hostility in everybody's eyes.

The My Lai story broke when I was over there. I just remember everybody saying, "Ah, number one, it didn't happen, it couldn't have happened, and number two, even if it did happen they deserved it. They're all the enemy. You know, babies and old women, they're all VC and deserve to die." It disgusted me back then and it still makes me angry and very, very sad. Maybe it's a universal trait to look away from your own ugliness. We Americans find it easy to be self-congratulatory about our country, but there's not a lot to congratulate ourselves about with regard to Vietnam.

Almost everybody I know who got out of the war somehow and stayed in the country says the same thing, almost to a man. They say, "Oh my God, I missed the great experience of my generation." They don't talk much about having done the right or wrong thing, they just seem to feel they missed out on something. I always say, "Well, you missed out on having your legs blown off and you missed out on having nightmares the rest of your life. You missed out on horror." They nod, but I can see they're thinking something else to themselves. They have a hard time articulating what it is they missed but it has to do with the American idea of manhood, with adventure, and with a gnawing sense of guilt. There's a guilt that not just Vietnam veterans, but the whole country carries around. I certainly don't relieve them of their guilt. I've got my own.

The Courage to Resist

I've gone to Canada for readings and met people who left the country during the war. A lot of these guys are embarrassed by it. They're asking the question today that they asked back then—did I do this because I was opposed to the war or because I didn't want to die? Was it cowardice or conscience? And that plagues all of us—those who went to Vietnam and those who went to Canada and those who just got out of it through legal means. It plagues everyone because no one wants to die, even in a right war. But there were a lot of us in Vietnam who didn't want to be there and many of us didn't have the courage to do what the resisters did. It took a lot of courage to cross the border and leave behind your family and your hometown and your girlfriend. What looked like an act of cowardice to the [President Ronald] Reagan-[Vice President Bob] Dole Republicans took a lot more courage than I had. Even though I was opposed to the war, I still couldn't find the courage to walk away. When I was at Fort Lewis before going to Vietnam, I planned to go to Vancouver. I came as close as you can come without actually doing it. I ended up going to Vietnam just to protect my reputation and sense of self-esteem, but the guys who went to Canada somehow were able to find the moral courage to make a choice they knew was gonna dog them the rest of their lives.

Placing the War in History

It stuns me how ignorant younger people are about the war, not just in high school, but college. They kind of know the music and they've seen [the Vietnam war film] *Apocalypse Now* or one of the other movies, but the actual issues that were at stake back then and remain at stake now, they know very little about. I don't think it's their fault so much as the teachers' or the curriculum. It's said to me all the time that school terms run out and they teach Vietnam in a day. And it's a lengthy, complex history! You have to go way back to really understand it.

I've had kids say to me, "*The Things They Carried* is the only book I've ever read." I say, "You mean about Vietnam?"

And they say, "No, I mean the first book I've read all the way through." It makes me feel pretty shitty because to understand my books you do have to know at least some of the history. Otherwise, what's all this doubt about that these characters have and what are they running away from and why do they think this is so horrible? Similarly, [Stephen Crane's war novel] *The Red Badge of Courage* would not be as rich and comprehensible if a reader knew nothing about the [American] Civil War. I just took it as a given in writing these books that people would know something of the history.

Vietnam and 9/11

The few times I've spoken since September 11 I've really pissed people off. In many ways, the events subsequent to September 11 remind me of the early stages of the Vietnam War. If you spoke up against our military response in Afghanistan, you were a Commie and a peacenik and a fag and that's a little how I felt after September 11. It's just so hard to speak up now. I'll give all the disclaimers, that I'm not for a moment condoning the attack on the World Trade Center and how it was obviously an evil act, but I also talk about how we always demonize our enemies as barbarians and madmen, as evil, pure and simple. Watching bin Laden and Bush is like watching two six-year-olds. One says you're an infidel, the other says you're evil. But that's not gonna get you anywhere. It forecloses the possibility of discussion. You can't talk with people you demonize. I say that and they're all over me.

O'Brien Is More than Just a Vietnam War Writer

Don Lee

Don Lee has taught at Macalester College and Temple University. He is the author of the novels Country of Origin *and* Wrack and Ruin *and the short-story collection* Yellow.

In this profile of Tim O'Brien, Don Lee describes how O'Brien's tenure in the army and service in Vietnam eventually led him to a career in writing. Like his father, he published his first pieces while serving in the army, and much of his early work centers on biographical combat experiences turned into fiction. But O'Brien is much more than a war writer. All of his books, Lee asserts, are love stories as much as they are war stories, which accounts for his popularity with both women and men readers. O'Brien's novels focus on what he describes as the twin themes of love and evil and the ways in which they intermingle.

In 1994, after his sixth book, *In the Lake of the Woods*, was released, [Tim O'Brien] distressed his many fans by vowing to stop writing fiction "for the foreseeable future." Then, a few months later, he published a now famous essay in *The New York Times Magazine* that described his return to Vietnam. With his girlfriend at the time, he visited My Lai, where on March 16, 1968, a company of American soldiers massacred an entire village in a matter of four hours—women, children, old men, chickens, dogs. The body count ranged from two to five hundred.

A Personal Crisis

From 1969–70, O'Brien had been an infantryman in the Quang Ngai province, and his platoon had been stationed in My Lai a year after the massacre. Then and now, he could feel

Don Lee, "About Tim O'Brien: A Profile," *Ploughshares*, 21/4–68, Winter 1995–1996, pp. 196–201. Reprinted by permission.

the evil in the place, "the wickedness that soaks into your blood and heats up and starts to sizzle." In the [*New York Times Magazine*] cover story, O'Brien elaborated on the complex associations of love and insanity that can boil over during a war, almost inevitably exploding into atrocity. But he went a step further, drawing parallels between the "guilt, depression, terror, shame" that infected both his Vietnam experience and his present life, especially [after] his girlfriend had left him. Chillingly, he admitted, "Last night suicide was on my mind. Not whether, but how." This time, his fans were not the only ones concerned. Friends and strangers alike called him: shrinks to sign him up, clergymen to save his soul, people who thought he had disclosed way too much, others who thought he had disclosed too little.

Today, O'Brien has no regrets about publishing the article. He considers it one of the best things he has ever written. "I reread it maybe once every two months," he says, "just to remind myself what writing's for. I don't mean catharsis. I mean communication. It was a hard thing to do. It saved my life, but it was a f--- of a thing to print." After taking nine months off and pulling his life back together, O'Brien started another novel, intrigued enough by the first page to write a second, propelled, as always, by his fundamental faith in the power of storytelling.

Hating the Vietnam War

Born in 1946, O'Brien was raised in small-town Minnesota, his father an insurance salesman, his mother an elementary school teacher. As a child, O'Brien was lonely, overweight, and a professed "dreamer," and he occupied himself by practicing magic tricks. For a brief time, he contemplated being a writer, inspired by some old clippings he'd found of his father's—personal accounts about fighting in Iwo Jima and Okinawa that had been published in *The New York Times* during World War II. When O'Brien entered college, however, his aspirations turned political. He was a political science major at Macalester [College in St. Paul, Minnesota], attended peace vigils and war protests, and planned to join the State Department to reform its policies. "I thought we needed people who were progressive and had the patience to try diplomacy instead of dropping bombs on people."

He never imagined he would be drafted upon graduation and actually sent to Vietnam. "I was walking around in a dream and repressing it all," he says, "thinking something would save my ass. Even getting on the plane for boot camp, I couldn't believe any of it was happening to me, someone who hated Boy Scouts and bugs and rifles." When he received his classification—not as a clerk, or a driver, or a cook, but as an infantryman—he seriously considered deserting to Canada. He now thinks it was an act of cowardice not to, particularly since he was against the war, but in 1969, as a twenty-two-year-old, he had feared the disapproval of his family and friends, his townspeople and country. He went to Vietnam and hated every minute of it, from beginning to end.

Publishing Career

When he came back to the States, he had a Purple Heart (he was wounded by shrapnel from a hand grenade) and several publishing credits. Much like his father, he had written personal reports about the war that had made their way into Minnesota newspapers, and while pursuing a doctorate at the Harvard School of Government, O'Brien expanded on the vignettes to form a book, *If I Die in a Combat Zone, Box Me Up and Ship Me Home*. He sent it first to Knopf, whose editors had high praise for the book. Yet they were already publishing a book about Vietnam, *Dispatches* by Michael Herr, and suggested that O'Brien try the editor Seymour Lawrence, who was in Boston. "He called me at my dormitory at Harvard," O'Brien recalls. "He said, 'Well, we're taking your book. Why don't you come over, I'll take you to lunch.' It was a big,

As a political science major at Macalester College in Minnesota (pictured), O'Brien regularly attended war protests and peace vigils. © Steve Skjold/Alamy.

drunken lunch at [the upscale restaurant] Trader Vic's in the old Statler Hilton [Hotel], during the course of which we decided to fire my agent. Sam said, 'Look, you're not going to get much money, there's no way, might as well fire the guy. Why give him ten percent?'"

If I Die in a Combat Zone was published in 1973, just as O'Brien was being hired as a national affairs reporter for *The Washington Post*, where he'd been an intern for two summers. "I didn't know the first thing about writing for a newspaper, but I learned fast," says O'Brien, who never took a writing workshop. The job helped tremendously in terms of discipline, which, O'Brien confesses, was a problem for him until then. "I learned the virtue of tenacity."

After his one-year stint at the *Post*, O'Brien simply wrote books. In 1975, he published *Northern Lights*, about two brothers—one a war hero, the other a farm agent who stayed home in Minnesota—who struggle to survive during a cross-country ski trip. *Going After Cacciato* came out in 1978. In the novel, an infantryman named Cacciato deserts, deciding to walk from Southeast Asia to Paris for the peace talks. Paul Berlin is ordered to capture Cacciato, and narrates an extended meditation on what might have happened if Cacciato had made it all the way to Paris. The novel won the National Book Award over John Irving's *The World According to Garp* and John Cheever's *Stories*.

The Nuclear Age, about a draft dodger turned uranium speculator who is obsessed with the threat of nuclear holocaust, was released in 1985, and then, in 1990, came *The Things They Carried*, which was a finalist for both the Pulitzer Prize and the National Book Critics Circle Award. The collection of interrelated stories revolves around the men of Alpha Company, an infantry platoon in Vietnam. The title story is a recitation of the soldiers' weapons and gear, the metaphorical mixing with the mundane: they carried M-60's and C rations and Claymores, and "the common scent of cowardice barely restrained, the instinct to run or freeze or hide, and in many respects this was the heaviest burden of all, for it could never be put down, it required perfect balance and perfect posture." A central motif in the book is the process of storytelling itself, the way imagination and language and memory can blur fact, and why "story-truth is truer sometimes than happening-truth."

Questions Without Answers

In his [1994] novel, *In the Lake of the Woods*, which is now in paperback, O'Brien takes this question of how much we can know about an event or a person one step further. John and Kathy Wade are staying at a secluded lakeside cottage in northern Minnesota. He has just lost a senatorial election by a landslide, after the revelation that he was among the soldiers at My Lai [a Vietnamese village in which American troops massacred hundreds of civilians], a fact he has tried to conceal from everyone—including his wife; even, pathologically, himself—for twenty years. A week after their arrival at the lake, Wade's wife disappears. Perhaps she drowned, perhaps she ran away, perhaps Wade murdered her. The mystery is never solved, and the lack of a traditional ending has produced surprisingly vocal reactions from readers.

"I get *calls* from people," O'Brien says. They ask questions, they offer their own opinions about what happened, they want to *know*, missing the point of the novel, that life often does not offer solutions or resolutions, that it is impossible to know completely what secrets lurk within people. As the anonymous narrator, who has conducted a four-year investigation into the case, comments in a footnote: "It's human nature. We are fascinated, all of us, by the implacable otherness of others. And we wish to penetrate by hypothesis, by daydream, by scientific investigation those leaden walls that encase the human spirit, that define it and guard it and hold it forever inaccessible. ('I love you,' someone says, and instantly we begin to wonder—'Well, how much?'—and when the answer comes—'With my whole heart'—we then wonder about the wholeness of a fickle heart.) Our lovers, our husbands, our wives, our fathers, our gods—they are all beyond us."

O'Brien feels strongly that *In the Lake of the Woods* is his best book to date, but it took its toll on him. He is a meticulous, some would say fanatical, craftsman. In general, he writes every day, all day. He does practically nothing else. He lifts weights, watches baseball, occasionally plays golf, and reads at night, but rarely ventures from his two-bedroom apartment near Harvard Square. He'll eke out the words, then discard them. It took him an entire year to finish nine pages of *The Nuclear Age*, although he tossed out thousands.

Always, it will begin with an image, "a picture of a human being doing something." With *Going After Cacciato*, it was the image of a guy walking to Paris: "I could see his back." With *The Things They Carried*, it was "remembering all this crap I had on me and inside me, the physical and spiritual burdens." With *In the Lake of the Woods*, it was a man and a woman lying on a porch in the fog along a lake: "I didn't know where the lake was at the time. I knew they were unhappy. I could feel the unhappiness in the fog. I didn't know what the unhappiness was about. It required me to write the next page. A lost election. Why was the election lost? My Lai. All of this was discovered after two years of writing."

But when O'Brien finished *In the Lake of the Woods*, he stopped writing for the first time in over twenty years. "I was burned out," he says. "The novel went to the bottom of the well for me. I felt emotionally drained. I didn't see the point of writing anymore." In retrospect, the respite was good for him. He likens the hiatus to [former NBA star] Michael Jordan's brief leave from basketball: "He may not be a better basketball player when he comes back, but he's going to be a better person."

More than a Vietnam War Writer

Of course, the road back has not been easy, particularly with the loss of his editor and good friend, Sam Lawrence, who died in 1993. "Through the ups and downs of any writer's career, he was always there, with a new contract, and optimism. Another of his virtues was that he didn't push. Sam didn't give a shit if you missed a deadline. He wanted a good book, no matter how long it took." For the moment, O'Brien has yet to sign up with another publisher for his novel in progress [*Tomcat in Love*], which opens with two boys building an airplane in their backyard. He prefers to avoid the pressure. "Maybe it's Midwestern," he says. "When I sign a contract, I think I owe them X dollars of literature."

And in defiance of some editors and critics, who suggest he should move on from Vietnam, he will in all likelihood continue to write about the war. "All writers revisit terrain. [William] Shakespeare did it with kings, and [Polish-born British novelist Joseph] Conrad did it with the ocean, and [American novelist William] Faulkner did it with the South. It's an emotional and geographical terrain that's given to us by life. Vietnam is there the way childhood is for me. There's a line from [*Dispatches* author] Michael Herr: 'Vietnam's what we had instead of happy childhoods.' A funny, weird line, but there's some truth in it."

Yet to categorize O'Brien as merely a Vietnam War writer would be ludicrously unfair and simplistic. Any close examination of his books reveals there is something much more universal about them. As much as they are war stories, they are also love stories. That is why his readers are as apt to be female as male. "I think in every book I've written," O'Brien says, "I've had the twins of love and evil. They intertwine and intermix. They'll separate, sometimes, yet they're hooked the way valances are hooked together. The emotions in war and in our ordinary lives are, if not identical, damn similar."

Applying Vietnam's Lessons to the Iraq War

Tim O'Brien, as told to Patrick Hicks

Patrick Hicks has taught creative writing at Augustana College in Sioux Falls, South Dakota. He is the author of the poetry collections Finding the Gossamer *and* This London.

In this interview with writer Patrick Hicks, Tim O'Brien discusses the Iraq War in the context of Vietnam, particularly in light of the war crimes that took place in Iraq. With regard to prisoner abuse at the Iraqi prison Abu Ghraib, O'Brien observes that war is inherently evil and the process of going to war will engender bad behavior. If the United States and other countries want to guard against the typical brutality and atrocities that are inevitable when they send young men out to kill others, they should not wage wars in the first place, O'Brien argues.

Tim O'Brien never intended to fight in the Vietnam War. In fact, after graduating *summa cum laude* from Macalester College in May 1968, he planned to study politics at Harvard. When the draft notice arrived in August of that same year, O'Brien reluctantly left his home in Minnesota and was assigned to the Quang Ngai Province of Vietnam, where he served with the 46th Infantry, 198th Infantry Brigade. O'Brien came to understand the soldierly experience with horrifying intimacy, and each night he wrote about what he saw. These foxhole scribblings are now lost, but the memory of Vietnam continues to burn throughout his writing.

After he returned to the United States in March 1970, O'Brien picked up where he left off. He went to Harvard, worked as a national affairs reporter for *The Washington Post*,

Patrick Hicks, "The *Progressive* Interview: Tim O'Brien," *Progressive*, 7-68, July 2004, pp. 37–40. Reprinted by permission.

and wrote his first book, *If I Die in a Combat Zone* (1973). This indictment against the war brought him immediate attention and launched his literary career. He is the author of six subsequent novels, including *Going After Cacciato* (1978), which received the National Book Award, and *The Things They Carried* (1990), which was a finalist for the Pulitzer Prize. He has also won the National Magazine Award, the O. Henry Award, and the Society of American Historians' Cooper Prize for best historical fiction. . . .

Abuse at Abu Ghraib

Patrick Hicks: The prison abuse scandal at [the Iraqi prison] Abu Ghraib has become a defining moment of the [Iraq] war. Are you surprised that prisoners were mistreated in Iraq?

Tim O'Brien: No, I'm not surprised in the least. I would have been surprised if they hadn't been mistreated. War is nasty and brings out the worst in people. Violence is sanctioned, and you're an eighteen-year-old kid, and nobody is overseeing you. The nastiness comes out. It was seen on a daily basis in Vietnam with prisoners. This was usually done by kids, and even if they were officers they were still only twenty-two or twenty-three years old. There is a disbelief that Americans could do this sort of thing, but it's a common occurrence in war.

You write about abuses by soldiers in your novel In the Lake of the Woods. *Do you think that abuses like Abu Ghraib can be prevented during times of war?*

Once you start making war, the consequences are, at least they seem to me, almost inevitable. I don't mean they can't be discouraged with good training and oversight—perhaps they can even be reduced in frequency—but I really don't think abuse like this can be entirely eliminated. If you don't like the nastiness of war, you shouldn't be making wars in the first place.

What effect do you think the prison scandal will have on our troops over there?

I think it will be sobering, if only in the sense that soldiers might be thinking to themselves, "Now we'd better be careful, keep it quiet, don't do it because we might be caught." It won't be avoided out of any sense of repulsion or outrage or horror.

From a Soldier's Perspective

Our soldiers have seen their medical benefits cut and their tours of duty extended. Aside from being demoralized by this, what else do you think might be going through their minds right now?

A sense of futility, because there is no front line, no rear, nowhere is it safe. It's much like what we saw in Vietnam. There's no happy ending. They're not aiming for Berlin or Tokyo with a sense of destination or goal.

What do you imagine the soldierly experience to be like over there?

No matter what the war—whether it's a glorious war like World War II or a stinky war like Vietnam—the facts are always the same when you're a soldier. There's death and horror and maiming and widows and orphans. Wars are all alike. The Crusades [religious military campaigns of the Middle Ages] were the same, I'm sure.

In a war, you're up against not just your own mortality, but you're up against a lifetime of memory. Wars don't end when you sign a peace treaty. They go on and on in memory. My friend Chip Merricks keeps soaring into a tree after he steps on a land mine. And he never stops going into that tree, and I never stop having to climb up and peel him off and throw him back down. It doesn't stop. That's what the guys in Iraq are up against. That's what wars in general are all about. They're about people going up one way, and coming back another way.

What type of war stories do you think our soldiers will be returning with from Iraq?

I think the stories will be very similar to what we returned with from Vietnam. Stories of confusion: Who's the enemy? And where are they? And how do we find them? Frustration. Anger. Watching all your friends die around you. An absence of clear purpose for it all. A sense of guilt for all the civilian casualties and the difficulty in finding the enemy.

The reason why we so overwhelmingly supported the Iraq War early on was to find weapons of mass destruction. We were terrified after 9/11 of anthrax and chemical weapons and nuclear weapons. And to find out that it was all inaccurate does something to a soldier because he's the person over there paying a price for this.

The Lessons of Vietnam

Do you think the United States has learned anything from Vietnam?

I thought so up until two years ago [2002]. You know, [American novelist] Kurt Vonnegut has this incredibly great line in *Slaughterhouse-Five* where someone asks if this is an anti-war book, and Vonnegut says, "I could no more write an anti-war book than an anti-glacier book." I'm starting to share that sad cynicism that we just don't learn. The answer is no, I don't believe we have. I'm starting to feel an uncanny sense of déjà vu. It's as if I'm watching the same headlines and the same story except now it's set in a desert world and not in a jungle world. Everything else seems very similar.

What lessons from Vietnam do you wish America had learned?

One is the quality of patience. We need to be more patient with the world. We have a quick-fix mentality. Usually through military means we think we'll repair the problems of the world, but real enduring fixes aren't quick because they require diplomacy and an understanding of history. Another lesson is underestimating the enemy's capacity for endurance.

We thought that if enough bombs were dropped, and enough people were killed, and enough infrastructure was destroyed, that would change the situation. It didn't work. We then doubled the tonnage of bombs, and that didn't work either. I don't think we learned that lesson at all. With the war in Iraq, we thought that by occupying it, and destroying an army, and overthrowing a regime, that all the pieces would fall tidily into place.

But there's no bright light at the end of this tunnel that I can see, and I don't think any soldier can see it either. After all, we've won the war, we've deposed Saddam [Hussein, former Iraqi leader], we've actually got him as our prisoner; and it's still not over. In fact, it's worse now that we've captured Saddam. And it's a lot worse, not just a little worse, a lot worse. What do we have to do to win? We've got the capital in our hands. What if we had taken Berlin and captured Hitler and the war was getting worse, not better? The objectives that the soldiers were given in Iraq have all been achieved, and yet it's not getting any better. The casualties are piling up, and frustration is climbing, and the citizenry of Baghdad—you can see the anger in their faces. These people were cheering us in the street not long ago as liberators. It's not that way anymore.

Are there other lessons we missed?

Yes. Another has to do with what happens when a bunch of white faces show up in a culture with few white faces. Even if it's not formally an occupation, it sure looks like one. Imagine a guy, a barber, some guy cutting hair in downtown Baghdad, and he watches a bunch of white faces go by with rifles. It feels like an occupation to him and it looks like one.

The Errors of Our Ways

Why did we forget the lessons of Vietnam?

It's part of our nature as a country. We look forward as a nation, and we tend to erase our flaws: like the genocide of the American Indians, and slavery, and Jim Crow laws [laws in effect between the 1880s and the 1960s designed to deprive African Americans of civil rights]. We forget these things, these flaws, these misdeeds. It's a part of our character for some reason to view ourselves with complacent rectitude.

I was talking in Texas at a school before the Iraq abuses came out. I talked about how our country was so upset about our soldiers being dragged through the streets of Mogadishu [in Somalia]. Yet when we displayed the corpses of Saddam Hussein's sons there was no outcry or disbelief. Some kid in the back of the room got really angry at me and said, "You can't compare American soldiers to the evil sons of Saddam Hussein." I tried to talk about [the massacre at the Vietnamese village] My Lai, what I'd witnessed, what American soldiers can do, but he just got up and walked out. He was really angry. And then this [Abu Ghraib scandal] comes up. On the one hand, I feel that my point has been made again, but on the other hand, I feel a sense of weariness about it all. When are we going to learn that we're as capable of evil as the next guy in the next country?

Do you think [President George W.] Bush, [Vice President Dick] Cheney, and [Secretary of Defense Donald] Rumsfeld knew what they were getting into with Iraq?

No, they thought they were going to go overthrow a bad guy and find some weapons of mass destruction, and set up a democracy, and then walk away. That's what they thought, more or less. There was some rhetoric about it taking time, but I don't think they anticipated the guerrilla warfare going on now.

Looking Ahead

Do you think it will get worse before it gets better?

Yes. The abuses of the prisoners are going to compound the outrage of the Iraqis who don't want us there in the first place. Every day that goes by I think it's just going to get worse, not better. . . .

Can you leave Vietnam behind and heal? Is that possible?

No, I don't believe in healing. I don't believe you heal from horror and evil. You deal with it, cope with it, pledge to do better. You try to learn and try to be more morally courageous. Healing is an inappropriate word. Some sores are best left open so that we don't forget, so that we learn and remember.

In the end, I'm a fiction writer, not a politician, and I'm trying to write stories that aren't about war, per se. They're not about bullets and bombs and military maneuvers and tactics; this stuff never interested me. But what does interest me is what happens to a human being's soul when stress is put on it, and not just physical stress but moral stress. Should I kill that person, or not? Should I go to war, or not? When is it right to say no to your politicians? Is it ever right? I don't have answers to any of these questions. All I have are a bunch of stories about human beings making their way through an uncertain world.

Social Issues in Literature

CHAPTER 2

War in *The Things They Carried*

O'Brien Makes His Peace with War

Robert R. Harris

Robert R. Harris has written for the New York Times *and served as an editor of the* New York Times Book Review.

The Things They Carried, in Robert R. Harris's estimation, is one of the few enduring fictional treatments of the Vietnam War. In the following viewpoint he argues that O'Brien's collection of interrelated stories depicts the war in a truthful manner, with all of its ugliness, obscenity, and shocking violence. According to O'Brien, if we send boys off to war, we must be prepared for the ugly consequences; but, telling war stories can help soldiers come to terms with their experience. For O'Brien, Harris explains, the war was an awful experience from beginning to end, and his an-tiwar book is, finally, about the human desire for peace.

Only a handful of novels and short stories have managed to clarify, in any lasting way, the meaning of the war in Vietnam for America and for the soldiers who served there. With *The Things They Carried*, Tim O'Brien adds his second title to the short list of essential fiction about Vietnam. As he did in his novel *Going After Cacciato* (1978), which won a National Book Award, he captures the war's pulsating rhythms and nerve-racking dangers. But he goes much further. By moving beyond the horror of the fighting to examine with sensitivity and insight the nature of courage and fear, by questioning the role that imagination plays in helping to form our memories and our own versions of truth, he places *The Things They Carried* high up on the list of best fiction about any war.

The Things They Carried is a collection of interrelated stories. A few are unremittingly brutal; a couple are flawed two-page sketches. The publisher calls the book "a work of fiction," but in no real sense can it be considered a novel. No matter. The stories cohere. All deal with a single platoon, one of whose members is a character named Tim O'Brien. Some stories are about the wartime experiences of this small group of grunts [foot soldiers]. Others are about a 43-year-old writer—again, the fictional character Tim O'Brien—remembering his platoon's experiences and writing war stories (and remembering writing stories) about them. This is the kind of writing about writing that makes [American novelist] Tom Wolfe grumble. It should not stop you from savoring a stunning performance. The overall effect of these original tales is devastating.

As might be expected, there is a lot of gore in *The Things They Carried*—like the account of the soldier who ties a friend's puppy to a Claymore antipersonnel mine and squeezes the firing device. And much of the powerful language cannot be quoted in a family newspaper. But let Mr. O'Brien explain why he could not spare squeamish sensibilities: "If you don't care for obscenity, you don't care for the truth; if you don't care for the truth, watch how you vote. Send guys to war, they come home talking dirty."

Too Embarrassed Not to Kill

In the title story, Mr. O'Brien juxtaposes the mundane and the deadly items that soldiers carry into battle. Can openers, pocketknives, wristwatches, mosquito repellent, chewing gum, candy, cigarettes, salt tablets, packets of Kool-Aid, matches, sewing kits, C rations are "humped" by the G.I.'s along with M-16 assault rifles, M-60 machine guns, M-79 grenade launchers. But the story is really about the other things the soldiers "carry": "grief, terror, love, longing . . . shameful memories" and, what unifies all the stories, "the common secret of cowardice." These young men, Mr. O'Brien tells us, "carried the soldier's greatest fear, which was the fear of blushing. Men killed, and died, because they were embarrassed not to."

Embarrassment, the author reveals in "On the Rainy River," is why he, or rather the fictional version of himself, went to Vietnam. He almost went to Canada instead. What stopped him, ironically, was fear. "All those eyes on me," he writes, "and I couldn't risk the embarrassment. . . . I couldn't endure the mockery, or the disgrace, or the patriotic ridicule. . . . I was a coward. I went to the war."

So just what is courage? What is cowardice? Mr. O'Brien spends much of the book carefully dissecting every nuance of the two qualities. In several stories, he writes movingly of the death of Kiowa, the best-loved member of the platoon. In "Speaking of Courage," Mr. O'Brien tells us about Norman Bowker, the platoon member who blames his own failure of nerve for Kiowa's death. Bowker "had been braver than he ever thought possible, but . . . he had not been so brave as he wanted to be." In the following story, "Notes" (literally notes on the writing of "Speaking of Courage"), Mr. O'Brien's fictional alter ego informs the reader that Bowker committed suicide after coming home from the war. This author also admits that he made up the part about the failure of nerve that haunted Bowker. But it's all made up, of course. And in "The Man I Killed," Mr. O'Brien imagines the life of an enemy soldier at whom the character Tim O'Brien tossed a grenade, only to confess later that it wasn't "Tim O'Brien" who killed the Vietnamese.

Are these simply tricks in the service of making good stories? Hardly. Mr. O'Brien strives to get beyond literal descriptions of what these men went through and what they felt. He makes sense of the unreality of the war—makes sense of why he has distorted that unreality even further in his fiction—by turning back to explore the workings of the imagination, by probing his memory of the terror and fearlessly confronting the way he has dealt with it as both soldier and fiction writer. In doing all this, he not only crystallizes the Vietnam experience for us, he exposes the nature of all war stories.

The Truth About War

The character Tim O'Brien's daughter asks him why he continues to be obsessed by the Vietnam War and with writing about it. "By telling stories," he says, "you objectify your own experience. You separate it from yourself. You pin down certain truths." In "Good Form," he writes: "I can look at things I never looked at. I can attach faces to grief and love and pity and God. I can be brave. I can make myself feel again." You come away from this book understanding why there have been so many novels about the Vietnam War, why so many of Mr. O'Brien's fellow soldiers have turned to narrative—real and imagined—to purge their memories, to appease the ghosts.

Is it fair to readers for Mr. O'Brien to have blurred his own identity as storyteller-soldier in these stories? "A true war story is never moral," he writes in "How to Tell a True War Story." "It does not instruct, nor encourage virtue, nor suggest models of proper human behavior, nor restrain men from doing the things men have always done. If a story seems moral, do not believe it. If at the end of a war story you feel uplifted, or if you feel that some small bit of rectitude has been salvaged from the larger waste, then you have been made the victim of a very old and terrible lie. There is no rectitude whatsoever. There is no virtue. As a first rule of thumb, therefore, you can tell a true war story by its absolute and uncompromising allegiance to obscenity and evil." Mr. O'Brien cuts to the heart of writing about war. And by subjecting his memory and imagination to such harsh scrutiny, he seems to have reached a reconciliation, to have made his peace—or to have made up his peace.

The Ninth Infantry Division returns to their base camp in 1969. Sharing war stories helps soldiers come to terms with their experiences. AP Photo/Henri Huet.

Almost all the dramatic furnishings of *The Things They Carried*—characters, scenery, incidents—are embedded in the Vietnam War. But the book is not about Vietnam and not about war, Tim O'Brien said in a telephone interview from his home in Boxford, Mass. There are almost no Vietnamese in the book, none with names anyway, a reflection of ignorance among the soldiers, the 43-year-old writer said. Mr. O'Brien draws on his year in Vietnam, but the character named Tim O'Brien is "just a 21-year-old kid at war. I did not know the culture or the language. I was afraid of dealing with stereotypes. I did try once, with the Tim character, to imagine the life of the man I killed, and that was the nearest I could come."

Nor is there much war in *The Things They Carried*, and that too was typical. "It was like trying to pin the tail on the Asian donkey," Mr. O'Brien said, "but there was no tail and no donkey. In a year I only saw the living enemy once. All I saw were flashes from the foliage and the results, the bodies. In books or films it is desirable to have a climactic battle scene, but the world does not operate in those gross dramatic terms. In Vietnam there was a general aimlessness, not just in the physical sense, but beyond that in the moral and ethical sense."

So what's the book about? [In O'Brien's words:] "It is a writer's book on the effects of time on the imagination. It is definitely an antiwar book; I hated the war from the beginning. [The book] is meant to be about man's yearning for peace. At least I hope it is taken that way."

The Things They Carried Depicts the Moral Complexity of War

Marilyn Wesley

Marilyn Wesley has served as Cora M. Babcock Professor of English at Hartwick College in Oneonta, New York. She is the author of Refusal and Transgression in Joyce Carol Oates' Fiction *and* Violent Adventure: Contemporary Fiction by American Men.

In this viewpoint, Marilyn Wesley analyzes three stories from The Things They Carried—*the title story, "How to Tell a True War Story," and "Sweetheart of the Song Tra Bong"—to illustrate how Tim O'Brien constructs a morally complex portrait of the Vietnam War experience. By avoiding the traditional motifs of war stories, Wesley states, O'Brien insists on depicting the war as a complex, morally ambiguous experience that defies simplistic attempts to make sense of it. For Wesley, the central issue of* The Things They Carried *is the need to evaluate the war in moral terms. To do so, O'Brien must reject the simple notion that American forces were heroes and the Vietnamese were villains; instead, he must retell his stories, scrupulously examining the war and those who waged it.*

The title story of *The Things They Carried* invokes and revises two key devices of generic war fiction: the structure of dramatic action and the focal representation of the officer. Buried within this narrative is a conventional plot. A platoon of infantrymen from Alpha Company, led by Lieutenant Jimmy Cross, is on a mission to destroy Viet Cong [Commu-

Marilyn Wesley, "Truth and Fiction in Tim O'Brien's *If I Die in a Combat Zone* and *The Things They Carried*." *College Literature*. 29-2, Spring 2002, pp. 1–18. Reprinted by permission.

nist guerrillas in South Vietnam] "villes" and tunnels. The seventeen men—among them, Ted Lavender, Lee Strunk, Rat Kiley, Henry Dobbins, Mitchell Sanders, Dave Jensen, Norman Bowker, Kiowa, and Tim O'Brien, characters who recur throughout the collection—are especially uneasy when they discover a tunnel. Standard operating procedure demands that one of their number, chosen by lot, crawl inside and explore before they blow it up, a maneuver literally dangerous and psychologically unnerving. On the day of the story, Lee Strunk is unlucky enough to have to descend. The others, worried for him and uneasily aware of their own mortality, await his eventual reemergence. Although Strunk returns unscathed, Ted Lavender, the most frightened of the group, is later shot while urinating. A helicopter is summoned to remove his body, and the men respond to his death in a variety of ways: relief, humor, hysterical grief, and the destruction of the nearby village of Than Khe.

The Burden of War

This imposed dramatic structure of violation and resolution, which makes violent death and chaotic response comprehensible, is not adapted by the story, which is, instead, organized as lists of actual and emotional burdens toted by the soldiers. The things they carry include the accouterments [trappings] of war, such as steel helmets, which, O'Brien carefully notes, weigh 5 pounds; the particular objects of their military duties, the 23-pound M-60 of the machine gunner or the medic's bag of "morphine and plasma and malaria tablets and surgical tape and comic books . . . for a total weight of almost 20 pounds"; and the heavier load of fear and whatever the men rely on to cope with fear, like Ted Lavender's drugs, Kiowa's bible, and Jimmy Cross's love letters.

In *Writing War* [feminist author and literary critic Lynne] Hanley contends that modern military narratives are suffused with a "'secret unacknowledged elation' at the thought of war, with the conviction that war is exciting," and that this style of representation has promoted war as a desirable societal event. But by presenting violence in terms of burden rather than battle through deliberately non-dramatic structure, by stressing the continuous pressure of war rather than the climactic action of combat through the metaphor of weight to be borne, "The Things They Carried" deflates the excitement of traditional portrayal of the violence of the military adventure, and it deflects the ascription of moral purpose to the violent events of war.

Similarly, this story, which foregrounds the reactions of Lieutenant Jimmy Cross, obviates his reception as noble example. Jimmy fights the inexpressible fear the men share by obsessing about a girl he wants to love and substituting the banalities of her letters for the reality of Vietnam. After Lavender's death, Cross digs a foxhole and gives in to uncontrolled weeping. Finally, despite the rain, he burns the letters. Accepting the "blame" for his soldier's death, he resolves to be a leader, not a lover, "determined to perform his duties firmly and without negligence." He imagines himself, henceforth, an officer in the manner of [macho movie star] John Wayne: "if anyone quarreled or complained, he would simply tighten his lips and arrange his shoulders in the correct command posture. . . . He might just shrug and say, Carry on, then they would saddle up and form into a column and move on. . . ." Like the rest of the men, the lieutenant responds to the random violence in largely unproductive ways. He doesn't set any superior standard because, like the others, he can find no relevant standard to set.

Of course, Lavender's death cannot be explained or contained by Cross's pose of heroic responsibility any more than it can be relieved by the unit's destruction of the "chickens and dogs" and hootches of Than Khe. In "The Things They Carried," the unplottable violence of the Vietnam experience is structurally contrasted to the assimilable violence of war as popular fiction. In the space between these two opposed representations—experiential disorder, the way the events of war feel to the soldiers in the field, and fictive order, the way popular representations suggest they should respond—emerges the "truth" about Vietnam as a constant process of "humping" or carrying the impossible responsibility of power through a violent landscape.

Two Violent Scenes

The proper treatment of this truth, O'Brien suggests, is storytelling. Conditioned as we are to the designations of "fiction" and "non-fiction," it is easy to imagine that truth and stories are opposite categories. "How to Tell a True War Story," however, dissolves this relation to allow storytelling to emerge as the pursuit of provisional comprehension. Two scenes of graphic violence organize this effect. The first is the death of a young soldier who steps on a mine during a happy moment; the second is the destruction of a baby water buffalo by his best friend:

> 1. In the mountains that day, I watched Lemon turn sideways. He laughed and said something to Rat Kiley. Then he took a peculiar half-step, moving from the shade into bright sunlight, and the booby-trapped 105 round blew him into a tree. The parts were just hanging there, so Dave Jensen and I were ordered to shinny up and peel him off. I remember pieces of skin and something wet and yellow that must've been the intestines. The gore was horrible, and stays with me.

> 2. He stepped back and shot it through the front right knee. The animal did not make a sound. It went down hard, then got up again and Rat took careful aim and shot off an ear. He shot it in the hindquarters and in the little hump at its back. It wasn't to kill; it was to hurt. He put the rifle muzzle up against the mouth and shot the mouth away. Nobody

said much. The whole platoon stood there feeling all sorts of things, but there wasn't a great deal of pity for the water buffalo.

The passage continues in this vein. Rat shoots off the tail, then wounds the baby water buffalo in the ribs, the belly, the knee, the nose, and the throat. It is still living when one of the men kicks it, and the group finally dumps it into the village well.

It is impossible to read these two passages without placing them in a causal relationship that induces emotional and political interpretation. The juxtaposition of nature and death is especially shocking. In the first scene the sunlit American boy is wastefully decimated by a hidden explosive device. Rat Kiley and Curt Lemon have just been playing catch with a smoke bomb, turning war, for a few moments of pastoral innocence, into a carefree game. But the Vietnamese have, evidently, broken the rules. An invisible enemy, they not only kill Curt, but cruelly dismember him. Although presented as a kind of hero, Curt is reduced to a substance to be peeled off and scraped away. A similar ironic reversal, Curt's "wet" and "yellow" intestines are converted from organs of life to signifiers of death.

The second scene is, apparently, a direct result of the first. Rat chooses a symbol of Vietnamese innocence, the ubiquitous water buffalo, which is an emblem of the culture, not an agent of war, and a "baby" at that, to mimic Curt, who has been cast as the momentary emblem of youthful American guilelessness. The horrific attack on the body of the animal mimics his friend's fragmentation and evisceration. The biblical motto of vengeance, "an eye for an eye ...," is literally enacted in a narrative sequence meant to inscribe the sense of just retribution. Revenge, as [literary critic] David Whillock notes, is a common plot device in film treatments of the Vietnam war which attempt to impose the closure "that was not possible" in actuality. This text, however, will not let the imputed causal attributions stand. At the end of the account of

Curt Lemon's death, O'Brien appends a narrative interpolation: "But what wakes me up twenty years later is Dave Jensen singing 'Lemon Tree' as we threw down the parts." Dave's humor, probably a means of self-protection, nevertheless deflects an automatic assignment of blame. Similarly, previous details about some of Curt's playful "pranks" disrupt his reception as an innocent character. In the condoling letter Rat writes to Curt's sister he describes a terrifying incident he thinks of as funny: "On Halloween night, this hot spooky night, the dude paints up his body all different colors and puts on this weird mask and hikes over to a ville and goes trick-or-treating almost stark naked, just boots and balls and an M-16."

Ethical Complexity

As a conclusion to the description of Rat's actions, O'Brien condenses the general reaction of the men into another gnomic [short and concise] comment by Jensen: "'Amazing,' Dave Jensen kept saying. 'A new wrinkle. I never seen it before.'" The awful humor of Jensen's song and his appreciative acknowledgement of the peculiar novelty of Rat's performance both undercut the causal efficacy of the sequence, which is, in fact, denied sequentiality by its placement within a fiction organized as an essay on writing the war story. And even while reacting with shock and sadness to the extensive catalogue of assaults on the body parts of the baby water buffalo, a reader may respond with irreverence to the exaggeration of the attenuated murder, an unwilling recognition of the kind of overstatement that signals a gag rather than a tragedy. This subversion of narrative causality is further reinforced as O'Brien alternates accounts of action with lectures on the postmodern tests of a "true war story" "How to Tell . . ." exemplifies: it cannot moralize or generalize, it will probably be obscene and most certainly embarrassing, and it will overturn convictions by muddling oppositional categories of truth and fiction, good and evil, and love and war. The effect of the true war story will be to replace certainty with confusion.

As parallel scenes of descriptive violence, the deaths of Curt Lemon and the baby water buffalo are meant to suggest opposed explications of guilt and innocence. But the postmodern sabotage of the codes of reception of these scenes confronts the complexity of moral responsibility, which the conventional war story may evade through the narrative attribution of cause and effect. In "The Things They Carried" Mitchell Sanders contends that the events of that story imply "a definite moral." When another soldier responds that he cannot extrapolate a meaning—"I don't see no moral," he insists—Sanders counters, "There it *is* man." The contrasting presentations of thematic and formal violence in "How to Tell a True War Story"—evocative description set against subversive representation—substitute ethical uncertainty for the accessible "moral" of traditional story-telling.

O'Brien also gives Mitchell Sanders the last word on the slaughter of the water buffalo: "'Well that's Nam,' he said. 'Garden of Evil. Over here, man, every sin's fresh and original.'" For [literary critic] R.W.B. Lewis the quintessential American story begins with a renovated Adam in the "Garden of Innocence" located in the geographic region he imagines is a "new" world, a mythic assumption O'Brien disputes in "Sweetheart of the Song Tra Bong." Lewis's Adam is the "hero of a new adventure: an individual emancipated from history . . . standing alone, self-reliant, and self-propelling, ready to confront whatever awaited." However, O'Brien's protagonists' participation in the violence of Vietnam serves to undermine such self-serving illusions of originality, confident self-control, as well as innocence.

For [literary critic] Tobey C. Herzog, in *Vietnam Stories: Innocence Lost,* the traditional theme of the initiation of a military protagonist into the depravity of war dominates central texts of literature on Vietnam, a premise O'Brien's fiction significantly complicates. The narrative of war, according to [literary historian] Paul Fussell's study [of World War I] *The*

Great War and Modern Memory, proceeds in three mythic stages: 1) "preparation" for war, usually based on inappropriate romanticized models; 2) participation in battle, which is "characterized by disenchantment and loss of innocence"; and 3) the resultant "consideration" of the experience of war. O'Brien's representation of the Vietnam War differs from this pattern, first, in that there is never innocence to be lost. In all three of his accounts—the memoir [*If I Die in a Combat Zone*], his novel *Going After Cacciato* (1978), and in *The Things They Carried*—the main character cooperates with the government despite his ethical objections to the Vietnamese conflict because of an inability to face social opprobrium if he does not do so. "It's not a happy ending," the narrator of "On the Rainy River" confides, "I was a coward, I went to the war." Secondly, O'Brien departs from Fussell's schema in that the dehumanizing preparation for the war in the boot camp in *If I Die* is coextensive with, not different from, the war itself; for O'Brien the war in Vietnam is the exaggeration of his nation's basic principles.

"Sweetheart of the Song Tra Bong"

Certainly *The Things They Carried*, like the World War I literature Fussell examined, evaluates the experience of war, but O'Brien's evaluation is less decisive and more inclusive. According to [American literary critic] Wayne Miller, in stories of the Great War [World War I] the conclusion emerges that it is the social system, not the soldier, that is blameworthy: in "a world in which traditional political and social values have lost meaning . . . one seeks one's separate peace." Although outraged by war, the literary doughboy [infantryman] emerges morally intact. The contemplation of violence in the "Sweetheart of the Song Tra Bong," however, does not allow the soldier the illusions of separation from a morally deficient culture or abdication of personal responsibility. . . .

In "Sweetheart of the Song Tra Bong," O'Brien inserts an innocent American girl between [the] twin idylls of denial and endorsement. Scripting an apocryphal military daydream, O'Brien has one of the young medics transport his seventeen-year-old girlfriend from the States to the war. The point of the story is not just that Mary Anne Bell—"this cute blonde just out of high school"—loses her innocence, but that her loss speaks to the general ethical confusion of the war in Vietnam.

According to Rat Kiley, who narrates her story, Mary Anne's transformation typifies that of any participant in the war. She begins her visit filled with dreams and goals dictated by American values: "someday they would be married and live in a fine gingerbread house near Lake Erie, and have three healthy yellow-haired children, and grow old together, and no doubt die in each other's arms and be buried in the same walnut casket. That was the plan." Soon, however, the young woman begins to change. Her immitigable curiosity leads her into contact with the Vietnamese countryside and the practices and procedures of both the camp's medics and its resident green berets [an elite fighting unit]. By the end of the second week she has begun to help treat the wounded and later begins to learn the tricks of the military trade. As a result of her new experience, Mary Anne begins to change: "she fell into the habits of the bush. No cosmetics, no fingernail filing. She stopped wearing jewelry, cut her hair short and wore it in a green bandanna." More important than the physical modification is the girl's characterological transformation. She doesn't laugh as often, her voice seems to deepen as she talks less but more forcefully, and even her face takes on a "new composure, almost serene, the fuzzy blue eyes narrowing into a tight, intelligent focus." Mary Anne no longer expresses the same expectations for the future with her lover, whom she leaves in order to participate in the *Apocalypse Now*–type military exploits [after the Francis Ford Coppola film] of the "Greenies" [green berets]. Finally, she leaves them, too, crossing "to the other side. She was part of the land. She was wearing her culottes, her pink sweater, and a necklace of human tongues. She was dangerous. She was ready for the kill."

Turning the archetypal tale of a young man's initiation into the male mystery of violence into the story of a young girl on a whimsical visit opens it to fresh interpretation. The first explanation supplied by the narrator follows Fussell's model of the conversion of innocence to experience: "What happened to her . . . was what happened to all of them. You come over clean and you get dirty and then afterward it's never the same." Thus, in a single stroke, O'Brien demolishes the masculine mystique of the violence of war as the litmus test for manhood. But there are deeper implications. Mary Anne's transformation is the consequence of an appeal that varies among Americans in Vietnam in intensity, but not in kind. She is presumably particularly vulnerable because her circumscribed feminine role as the archetypal American girl-next-door has not allowed her any previous access to "the adrenaline buzz" of the operating theater nor the narcotic "high" of the battlefield: "you become intimate with danger; you're in touch with the far side of yourself," like "the effect of a powerful drug: that mix of unnamed terror and unnamed pleasure that comes as the needle slips in." . . . O'Brien offers an analytic depiction of its appeal that functions, as well, as a powerful critique of normative American values. Besides the rejection of war as masculine ritual, "Sweetheart of the Song Tra Bong" posits a kind of falseness of national experience, especially true of feminine socialization, that accounts for the addictive appeal of the existential authenticity encountered in the danger and physical extremes imposed by war. Mary Anne's induction into genuine experience is clearly destructive as well as empowering. That she, or any other American, can only encounter personal potential and visionary "truth" in the national practice of institutionalized death is the story's most disturbing implication. When she accuses her boyfriend of insularity, she expresses a key ethical argument of *The Things They Carried*: "You hide in this little fortress, behind wire and sandbags, and you don't know what it's all about." The concept of innocence—presented as the absence of the experience of moral complexity—is rejected as a legitimate basis for morality.

The Necessity of Moral Evaluation

In the war stories of *The Things They Carried* Tim O'Brien represents violence in terms of opposing narrative possibilities: the unplottable experience contrasting the implicit order of "The Things They Carried," the narrative sequence and the postmodern dislocation of "How to Tell a True War Story," the containing and exploiting myths invoked in "Sweetheart of the Song Tra Bong." What emerges is not another ameliorating instance of the "loss of innocence"—war imagined as something imposed on soldiers rather than enacted by them (and us)—nor even a clarification of what is right and wrong. The first story introduces the moral burden of war; the second insists on the provisional nature of the process of ethical inquiry; and the third deconstructs the categories through which such judgments are conventionally assigned: guilt and innocence, self and other, male and female. O'Brien's contradictory depictions of violence produce the thematic assertion of the moral confusion imposed by the war, and his manipulations of textual conventions violate the comfortable reception of war modeled by its traditional depiction as a test of courage, a mode of heroism, or an assertion of superiority or virtue. Instead, O'Brien's representational divergence demands the possibly impossible ethical interrogation of the violence of Vietnam.

Like Dave Jensen, the soldier amazed by the originality of experience in Vietnam, critics have been astounded by O'Brien's apparent newness. His narratives of war have been variously labeled as postmodern; magic realism; "faction," a combination of fact and fiction; even "fictive irrealism." But these metafictive [referring to fiction that is about the writing of fiction] labels stress his stunning epistemological [related to how we understand reality] effects at the expense of his troubling ethical achievement. In "The Vietnam in Me," an essay published in 1994 on the twenty-fifth anniversary of his tour of duty, he emphasizes the disturbing moral legacy of the American war in Vietnam. In addition to revealing the painful symptoms of his own continuing confusion—isolation, nightmares, depression, suicidal impulses—O'Brien expresses his outrage at the massacre at My Lai by soldiers of Charlie Company on March 16, 1968, two years before he served in the same region. But he reserves his severest condemnation for the moral abdication of the US in reaction to such incidents:

> I despised everything—the soil, the tunnels, the paddies, the poverty and myself. Each step was an act of the purest self-hatred and self-betrayal, yet, in truth, because truth matters, my sympathies were rarely with the Vietnamese. I was mostly terrified. I was lamenting in advance my own pitiful demise. After firefights, after friends died, there was a great deal of anger—black, fierce, hurting anger—the kind you want to take out on whatever presents itself. This is not to justify what occurred. . . . Justifications are empty and outrageous. Rather, it's to say that I more or less understand what happened on that day in March 1968, how it happened, the wickedness that soaks into your blood and heats up and starts to sizzle. I know the boil that precedes butchery. At the same time, however, the men in Alpha company [the unit in which O'Brien served] did not commit murder. We did not turn our machine guns on civilians; we did not cross that conspicuous line between rage and homicide. I know what occurred here, yes, but I also feel betrayed by a nation that so widely shrugs off barbarity, by a military justice system that treats murderers and common soldiers as one and the same. Apparently we're all innocent—those who exercise moral restraint and those who do not, officers

who control their troops and officers who do not. In a way America has declared *itself* innocent.

It is the absolute necessity of moral evaluation that is the central issue of *The Things They Carried*. The moral certainty that assigns absolute righteousness to "us" and complete culpability to "them"—the object of the war narrative [literary theorist Elaine] Scarry describes [in her study *The Body in Pain*]—is precisely what O'Brien's strategic sabotage of textual certainty in *The Things They Carried* is meant to forestall. For it is only through the unflinching willingness to evade the consoling simplicity built in to the formulaic war narrative process that genuine responsibility can be attempted. And for O'Brien, author of the war stories in *If I Die in a Combat Zone* and *Going After Cacciato*, as well as those of *The Things They Carried*, it is the telling, the retelling of war stories that leads to the possibility of the scrupulous analysis to which he is committed: "All you can do is tell it one more time, patiently, adding and subtracting, making up a few things to get at the real truth," which is a truth not just of texture but of accountability.

The Things They Carried
Contains Fictitious Truths

Steven Kaplan

Steven Kaplan has served as English Department chair at the University of Southern Colorado, dean of the College of Liberal Arts at Butler University, chancellor of the University of Virginia's College at Wise, and president of the University of New Haven. He is the author of Understanding Tim O'Brien.

In the following selection, Steven Kaplan begins by calling attention to how other literary works about Vietnam make the point that the only thing certain about the war was uncertainty. O'Brien reinforces this notion in The Things They Carried, *Kaplan writes, by laying out the specifics of the war—as in the opening story, when he factually recounts the items soldiers carried—and then undercutting many of these "facts" as the story progresses. O'Brien continually insists in his book that his audience is reading the full and exact truth, and yet subsequent stories reveal the fictitiousness of these tales. In this way, a work of fiction may be more real than the supposed reality it is based on, because the exact truths of Vietnam are hazy and ambiguous at best. But each time the stories are retold, Kaplan asserts, the events and characters come alive once more. In this manner, readers get as close to the actual truths of Vietnam as they are likely to come.*

Before the United States became militarily involved in defending the sovereignty of South Vietnam, it had to, as [historian Loren Baritz] recently put it, "invent" the country and the political issues at stake there. The Vietnam War was in many ways a wild and terrible work of fiction written by some

Steven Kaplan, "The Undying Uncertainty of the Narrator in Tim O'Brien's *The Things They Carried.*" *Critique: Studies in Contemporary Fiction*, 35-1, Fall 1993, pp. 43–52. Reprinted by permission.

dangerous and frightening storytellers. First the United States decided what constituted good and evil, right and wrong, civilized and uncivilized, freedom and oppression for Vietnam, according to American standards; then it traveled the long physical distance to Vietnam and attempted to make its own notions about these things clear to the Vietnamese people— ultimately by brute, technological force. For the U.S. military and government, the Vietnam that they had in effect invented became fact. For the soldiers that the government then sent there, however, the facts that their government had created about who was the enemy, what were the issues, and how the war was to be won were quickly overshadowed by a world of uncertainty. Ultimately, trying to stay alive long enough to return home in one piece was the only thing that made any sense to them. As [American author] David Halberstam puts it in his novel, *One Very Hot Day*, the only fact of which an American soldier in Vietnam could be certain was that "yes was no longer yes, no was no longer no, maybe was more certainly maybe." Almost all of the literature on the war, both fictional and nonfictional, makes clear that the only certain thing during the Vietnam War was that nothing was certain. [Scholar] Philip Beidler has pointed out in an impressive study of the literature of that war that "most of the time in Vietnam, there were some things that seemed just too terrible and strange to be true and others that were just too terrible and true to be strange."

The main question that Beidler's study raises is how, in light of the overwhelming ambiguity that characterized the Vietnam experience, could any sense or meaning be derived from what happened and, above all, how could this meaning, if it were found, be conveyed to those who had not experienced the war? The answer Beidler's book offers, as Beidler himself recently said at a conference on writing about the war, is that "words are all we have. In the hands of true artists . . . they may yet preserve us against the darkness." Similarly, for

By factually recounting the items soldiers carried—dog tags and specific gun models—and then undercutting many of these "facts," Tim O'Brien illustrates the hazy truths surrounding the Vietnam War. Library of Congress.

the novelist Tim O'Brien, the language of fiction is the most accurate means for conveying, as Beidler so incisively puts it, "what happened (in Vietnam) . . . what might have happened, what could have happened, what should have happened, and maybe also what can be kept from happening or what can be made to happen." If the experience of Vietnam and its accompanying sense of chaos and confusion can be shown at all, then for Tim O'Brien it will not be in the fictions created by politicians but in the stories told by writers of fiction. . . .

Fact Versus Fiction

In his most recent work of fiction, *The Things They Carried*, Tim O'Brien takes the act of trying to reveal and understand the uncertainties about the war one step further [than he did in earlier works] by looking at it through the imagination. He completely destroys the fine line dividing fact from fiction and tries to show, even more so than in [his novel *Going After*]

Cacciato, that fiction (or the imagined world) can often be truer, especially in the case of Vietnam, than fact. In the first chapter, an almost documentary account of the items referred to in the book's title, O'Brien introduces the reader to some of the things, both imaginary and concrete, emotional and physical, that the average foot soldier had to carry through the jungles of Vietnam. All of the "things" are depicted in a style that is almost scientific in its precision. We are told how much each subject weighs, either psychologically or physically, and, in the case of artillery, we are even told how many ounces each round weighed:

> As PFCs [privates first class] or Spec 4s [specialists fourth class], most of them were common grunts and carried the standard M-16 gas operated assault rifle. The weapon weighed 7.5 pounds, 8.2 pounds with its full 20-round magazine. Depending on numerous factors, such as topography and psychology, the rifleman carried anywhere from 12 to 20 magazines, usually in cloth bandoliers, adding on another 8.4 pounds at minimum, 14 pounds at maximum.

Even the most insignificant details seem worth mentioning. One main character is not just from Oklahoma City but from "Oklahoma City, Oklahoma," as if mentioning the state somehow makes the location more factual, more certain. More striking than this obsession with even the minutest detail, however, is the academic tone that at times makes the narrative sound like a government report. We find such transitional phrases as "for instance" and "in addition," and whole paragraphs are dominated by sentences that begin with "because." These strengthen our impression that the narrator is striving, above all else, to convince us of the reality, of the concrete certainty, of the things they carried.

The Uncertainty of the Soldier

In the midst of this factuality and certainty, however, are signals that all the information in this opening chapter will not amount to much: that the certainties are merely there to conceal uncertainties and that the words following the frequent "because" do not provide an explanation of anything. We are told in the opening page that the most important thing that First Lieutenant Jimmy Cross carried were some letters from a girl he loved. The narrator, one of Cross's friends in the war and now a forty-three-year-old writer named Tim O'Brien, tells us that the girl did not love Cross, but that he constantly indulged in "hoping" and "pretending" in an effort to turn her love into fact. We are also told "she was a virgin," but this is immediately qualified by the statement that "he was almost sure" of this. On the next page, Cross becomes increasingly uncertain as he sits at "night and wonder(s) if Martha was a virgin." Shortly after this, Cross wonders who had taken the pictures he now holds in his hands "because he knew she had boyfriends," but we are never told how he "knew" this. At the end of the chapter, after one of Cross's men has died because Cross was too busy thinking of Martha, Cross sits at the bottom of his foxhole crying, not so much for the member of his platoon who has been killed "but mostly it was for Martha, and for himself, because she belonged to another world, and because she was . . . a poet and a virgin and uninvolved."

This pattern of stating facts and then quickly calling them into question that is typical of Jimmy Cross's thoughts in these opening pages characterizes how the narrator portrays events throughout this book: the facts about an event are given; they then are quickly qualified or called into question; from this uncertainty emerges a new set of facts about the same subject that are again called into question—on and on, without end. O'Brien catalogues the weapons that the soldiers carried, down to their weight, thus making them seem important and their protective power real. However, several of these passages are introduced by the statement that some of these same weapons were also carried by the character Ted Lavender; each of the four sections of the first chapter that tells us what he carried is introduced by a qualifying phrase that reveals something about which Lavender himself was not at all certain when he was carrying his weapons: "Until he was shot . . ."

Conveying the average soldier's sense of uncertainty about what actually happened in Vietnam by presenting the what-ifs and maybes as if they were facts, and then calling these facts back into question again, can be seen as a variation of the haunting phrase used so often by American soldiers to convey their own uncertainty about what happened in Vietnam: "there it is." They used it to make the unspeakable and indescribable and the uncertain real and present for a fleeting moment. Similarly, O'Brien presents facts and stories that are only temporarily certain and real; the strange "balance" in Vietnam between "crazy and almost crazy" always creeps back in and forces the mind that is remembering and retelling a story to remember and retell it one more time in a different form, adding different nuances, and then to tell it again one more time.

Truth in Storytelling

Storytelling in this book is something in which "the whole world is rearranged" in an effort to get at the "full truth" about events that themselves deny the possibility of arriving at something called the "full," meaning certain and fixed, "truth." By giving the reader facts and then calling those facts into question, by telling stories and then saying that those stories happened, and then that they did not happen, and then that they might have happened, O'Brien puts more emphasis in *The Things They Carried* on the question that he first posed in *Going After Cacciato:* how can a work of fiction become paradoxically more real than the events upon which it is based, and how can the confusing experiences of the average soldier in Vietnam be conveyed in such a way that they will acquire at least a momentary sense of certainty. In *The Things They*

Carried, this question is raised even before the novel begins. The book opens with a reminder: "This is a work of fiction. Except for a few details regarding the author's own life, all the incidents, names, and characters are imaginary." Two pages later we are told that "this book is lovingly dedicated to the men of Alpha Company, and in particular to Jimmy Cross, Norman Bowker, Rat Kiley, Mitchell Sanders, Henry Dobbins, and Kiowa." We discover only a few pages after this dedication that those six men are the novel's main characters.

These prefatory comments force us simultaneously to consider the unreal (the fictions that follow) as real because the book is dedicated to the characters who appear in it, and the "incidents, names, and characters" are unreal or "imaginary." O'Brien informs us at one point that in telling these war stories he intends to get at the "full truth" about them; yet from the outset he has shown us that the full truth as he sees it is in itself something ambiguous. Are these stories and the characters in them real or imaginary, or does the "truth" hover somewhere between the two? A closer look at the book's narrative structure reveals that O'Brien is incapable of answering the questions that he initially raises, because the very act of writing fiction about the war, of telling war stories, as he practices it in *The Things They Carried*, is determined by the nature of the Vietnam War and ultimately by life in general where "the only certainty is overwhelming ambiguity."

The emphasis on ambiguity behind O'Brien's narrative technique in *The Things They Carried* is thus similar to the pattern used by [Polish-born British novelist] Joseph Conrad's narrator, Marlow, in *Heart of Darkness*, so incisively characterized by [literary scholar] J. Hillis Miller as a lifting of veils to reveal a truth that is quickly obscured again by the dropping of a new veil. Over and over again, O'Brien tells us that we are reading "the full and exact truth," and yet, as we make our way through this book and gradually find the same stories being retold with new facts and from a new perspective, we come to realize that there is no such thing as the full and exact truth. Instead, the only thing that can be determined at the end of the story is its own indeterminacy.

O'Brien calls telling stories in this manner "Good Form" in the title of one of the chapters of *The Things They Carried*: This is good form because "telling stories" like this "can make things present." The stories in this book are not truer than the actual things that happened in Vietnam because they contain some higher, metaphysical truth: "True war stories do not generalize. They do not indulge in abstractions or analysis." Rather, these stories are true because the characters and events within them are being given a new life each time they are told and retold. . . .

In *The Things They Carried*, Tim O'Brien desperately struggles to make his readers believe that what they are reading is true because he wants them to step outside their everyday reality and participate in the events that he is portraying: he wants us to believe in his stories to the point where we are virtually in the stories so that we might gain a more thorough understanding of, or feeling for, what is being portrayed in them. Representation as O'Brien practices this book is not a mimetic act but a "game." . . .

In *The Things They Carried*, representation includes staging what might have happened in Vietnam while simultaneously questioning the accuracy and credibility of the narrative act itself. The reader is thus made fully aware of being made a participant in a game, in a "performative act," and thereby also is asked to become immediately involved in the incredibly frustrating act of trying to make sense of events that resist understanding. The reader is permitted to experience at first hand the uncertainty that characterized being in Vietnam. We are being forced to "believe" that the only "certainty" was the "overwhelming ambiguity."

Rat Kiley's "True" Story

This process is nowhere clearer than in a chapter appropriately called "How to Tell a True War Story." O'Brien opens this chapter by telling us "THIS IS TRUE." Then he takes us through a series of variations of the story about how Kurt Lemon stepped on a mine and was blown up into a tree. The only thing true or certain about the story, however, is that it is being constructed and then deconstructed and then reconstructed right in front of us. The reader is given six different versions of the death of Kurt Lemon, and each version is so discomforting that it is difficult to come up with a more accurate statement to describe his senseless death than "there it is." Or as O'Brien puts it—"in the end, really there's nothing much to say about a true war story, except maybe 'Oh.'"

Before we learn in this chapter how Kurt Lemon was killed, we are told the "true" story that Rat Kiley apparently told to the character-narrator O'Brien about how Kiley wrote to Lemon's sister and "says he loved the guy. He says the guy was his best friend in the world." Two months after writing the letter, Kiley has not heard from Lemon's sister, and so he writes her off as a "dumb cooze." This is what happened according to Kiley, and O'Brien assures us that the story is "incredibly sad and true." However, when Rat Kiley tells a story in another chapter we are warned that he

> swore up and down to its truth, although in the end, I'll admit, that doesn't amount to much of a warranty. Among the men in Alpha Company, Rat had a reputation for exaggeration and overstatement, a compulsion to rev up the facts, and for most of us it was normal procedure to discount sixty or seventy percent of anything he had to say.

Rat Kiley is an unreliable narrator, and his facts are always distorted, but this does not affect storytelling truth as far as O'Brien is concerned. The passage above on Rat Kiley's credibility as a storyteller concludes: "It wasn't a question of deceit. Just the opposite: he wanted to heat up the truth, to make it burn so hot that you would feel exactly what he felt." This summarizes O'Brien's often confusing narrative strategy in *The Things They Carried*: the facts about what actually happened, or whether anything happened at all, are not important. They cannot be important because they themselves are too uncertain, too lost in a world in which certainty had vanished somewhere between the "crazy and almost crazy." The important thing is that any story about the war, any "true war story," must "burn so hot" when it is told that it becomes alive for the listener-reader in the act of its telling. . . .

Uncertainty in All Events

O'Brien demonstrates nothing new about trying to tell war stories—that the "truths" they contain "are contradictory," elusive, and thus indeterminate. Two hundred years ago, [German writer Johann Wolfgang von] Goethe, as he tried to depict the senseless bloodshed during the allied invasion of revolutionary France, also reflected in his autobiographical essay *Campaign in France* on the same inevitable contradictions that arise when one speaks, of what happened or might have happened in battle. [Greek epic poet] Homer's *Illiad* is, of course, the ultimate statement on the contradictions inherent in war. However, what is new in O'Brien's approach in *The Things They Carried* is that he makes the axiom that in war "almost everything is true. Almost nothing is true" the basis for the act of telling a war story.

The narrative strategy that O'Brien uses in this book to portray the uncertainty of what happened in Vietnam is not restricted to depicting war, and O'Brien does not limit it to the war alone. He concludes his book with a chapter titled "The Lives of the Dead" in which he moves from his experiences in Vietnam back to when he was nine years old. On the surface, the book's last chapter is about O'Brien's first date, his first love, a girl named Linda who died of a brain tumor a few months after he had taken her to see the movie, *The Man*

Who Never Was. What this chapter is really about, however, as its title suggests, is how the dead (which also include people who may never have actually existed) can be given life in a work of fiction. In a story, O'Brien tells us, "memory and imagination and language combine to make spirits in the head. There is the illusion of aliveness." Like the man who never was in the film of that title, the people that never were except in memories and the imagination can become real or alive, if only for a moment, through the act of storytelling.

According to O'Brien, when you tell a story, really tell it, "you objectify your own experience. You separate it from yourself." By doing this you are able to externalize "a swirl of memories that might otherwise have ended in paralysis or worse." However, the storyteller does not just escape from the events and people in a story by placing them on paper; as we have seen, the act of telling a given story is an on-going and never-ending process. By constantly involving and then re-involving the reader in the task of determining what "actually" happened in a given situation, in a story, and by forcing the reader to experience the impossibility of ever knowing with any certainty what actually happened, O'Brien liberates himself from the lonesome responsibility of remembering and trying to understand events. He also creates a community of individuals immersed in the act of experiencing the uncertainty or indeterminacy of all events, regardless of whether they occurred in Vietnam, in a small town in Minnesota, or somewhere in the reader's own life.

The Writer Saving Himself

O'Brien thus saves himself, as he puts it in the last sentence of his book, from the fate of his character Norman Bowker who, in a chapter called "Speaking of Courage," kills himself because he cannot find some lasting meaning in the horrible things he experienced in Vietnam. O'Brien saves himself by demonstrating in this book that the most important thing is to be able to recognize and accept that events have no fixed or final meaning and that the only meaning that events can have is one that emerges momentarily and then shifts and changes each time that the events come alive as they are remembered or portrayed.

The character Norman Bowker hangs himself in the locker room of the local YMCA after playing basketball with some friends partially because he has a story locked up inside of himself that he feels he cannot tell because no one would want to hear it. It is the story of how he failed to save his friend, Kiowa, from drowning in a field of human excrement: "A good war story, he thought, but it was not a war for war stories, not for talk of valor, and nobody in town wanted to know about the stink. They wanted good intentions and good deeds." Bowker's dilemma is remarkably similar to that of [protagonist Harold] Krebs in [writer Ernest] Hemingway's story "Soldier's Home": "At first Krebs . . . did not want to talk about the war at all. Later he felt the need to talk but no one wanted to hear about it. His town had heard too many atrocity stories to be thrilled by actualities."

O'Brien, after his war took on the task "of grabbing people by the shirt and explaining exactly what had happened to me." He explains in *The Things They Carried* that it is impossible to know "exactly what had happened." He wants us to know all of the things he/they/we did not know about Vietnam and will probably never know. He wants us to feel the sense of uncertainty that his character/narrator Tim O'Brien experiences twenty years after the war when he returns to the place where his friend Kiowa sank into a "field of shit" and tries to find "something meaningful and right" to say but ultimately can only say, "well . . . there it is." Each time we, the readers of *The Things They Carried*, return to Vietnam through O'Brien's labyrinth of stories, we become more and more aware that this statement is the closest we probably ever will come to knowing the "real truth," the undying uncertainty of the Vietnam War.

O'Brien Blurs the Line Between Fact and Fiction

Don Ringnalda

Don Ringnalda taught English at the University of St. Thomas in St. Paul, Minnesota.

Readers of The Things They Carried *are often uneasy about O'Brien's creation of a hybrid book that is part nonfiction and part fiction and about O'Brien's deliberate ambiguity concerning what is fact and what is not. Don Ringnalda sees this ambiguity as a parallel to the war itself. The United States, believing itself to be in the right in its struggle against Communist aggression, entered the war with high-minded principles that were in themselves fictions. Ringnalda compares the blurriness of everything associated with the Vietnam War to O'Brien's abortive attempt to escape the war by fleeing to Canada. In his story "On the Rainy River," O'Brien describes not knowing where the United States stopped and Canada began; while boating on the river, he may actually have crossed into Canada without realizing it. This uncertainty pervades* The Things They Carried *and the Vietnam War as a whole, Ringnalda suggests, and readers who demand certainty from O'Brien's book are missing the point.*

I first delivered my thoughts on *The Things They Carried* in a paper at an academic conference. Because the book had not yet been published, and because most people had at best read only the essay-like "The Things They Carried" and "How to Tell a True War Story," both serialized in [the magazine] *Esquire*, my panel was designated "Nonfiction Representations of the Vietnam War." Even though I recognize that session titles often are somewhat arbitrary because of the scores of papers

Don Ringnalda, "Tim O'Brien's Understood Confusion," *Fighting and Writing the Vietnam War*, University Press of Mississippi, 1994, pp. 100–04. Reprinted by permission.

being delivered, this designation, at the very least, suggests that we try to put our foot-occupied boot back on; it implies that we're confident of the difference between nonfiction and fiction, that despite what Vietnam should have taught us, we steadfastly remain a genre-sure country. I maintain that this genre-sureness got us into Vietnam in the first place. Not recognizing the powerful influence of our positivistic paradigm [what we see as an objective reality], we simply didn't—and still don't—see our "essays" as fictions. In its righteous, anti-Communist paradigm, it wasn't just that America "forgot who wrote the play"; it forgot that it was acting.

Ambiguities of War

This has resulted in a lot of wasted time and suffering and has prevented us from studying the machinery of observation itself. O'Brien is not at all sure of the strength of the walls erected by clear-cut genre distinctions. A number of the separately published chapters of [*The Things They*] *Carried* dissolve the wall separating essay and fiction. We often find ourselves in what O'Brien calls the "no-man's land between" the two, "between Cleveland Heights and deep jungle." We "come up on the edge of something" and "swirl back and forth across the border."

In the chapter entitled "On the Rainy River," O'Brien provides a geographical analogue for his genre-straddling. After receiving his draft notice in Worthington, Minnesota, he flees north to the Rainy River, located on the U.S.-Canada border. While staying at the Tip Top Lodge, for six days he vacillates [wavers] in anguish—cowardice or bravery, Canada or Vietnam? On one occasion he literally vacillates while fishing on the river. He says "at some point we must've passed into Canadian waters, across that dotted line between two different worlds." Because the "dotted line" at times is on the river itself, it's not that O'Brien is on a body of water that neatly separates two land masses; instead, carried by currents and eddies on a snaking river in the middle of a wilderness domi-nated by "great sweeps of pine and birch and sumac," he can't tell which country he is in.

This geographical ambiguity directly corresponds to his liminal [on a threshold between states or conditions] uncer-tainty. He understands that the old man running the boat has taken him to a wavering edge. But he says ". . . what embar-rasses me . . . and always will, is the paralysis that took my heart. A moral freeze. I couldn't decide, I couldn't act. . . ." Even when he does decide on one shore or the other, he in-verts what for many people would be a common-sense inter-pretation of fleeing to or not fleeing to Canada: "I would not swim away from my hometown and my country and my life. I would not be brave." . . .

Blurring Fact and Fiction

It is precisely because of his liminal uncertainty that the au-thor could not make *Carried* memoir or fiction, essay or story, autobiography or metafiction [fiction about fiction], no more than he knew while on the Rainy River if he was in the United States or Canada. The line separating genres is at most a dot-ted, wavering one. Like "Nuoc Vietnam" [a name for Vietnam that means "water nation"]. It's watery. Moving from *If I Die* [*in a Combat Zone*, O'Brien's memoir], to [his novel, *Going After*] *Cacciato*, to *Carried*, O'Brien seems to have developed an ever-finer appreciation of how fact and fiction interpen-etrate one another, and how the ultimate fiction is the belief that fiction is one thing, reality quite another. In fact, I'm cer-tain O'Brien would agree with me that because America was blinded to the fictionality of its "essay," it was, as I've sug-gested, self-lured into the Vietnam quagmire. In its genre cockiness, America was epistemologically [in regard to the scope of its knowledge] crude and naive. O'Brien's genius is that in the face of his wonderment he has found a way to take advantage of "a new understanding of [his] confusion." More sophisticated epistemologically than most Vietnam writers, O'Brien is able to pilot the reader through the shifting contours, eddies, and currents of the imagination.

I once had the opportunity to witness O'Brien's piloting skills, and the reaction of people who are suddenly made aware that they're on the Rainy River, not terra firma. It's akin to lifting the mostly empty milk carton that you think is full. Shortly before *Carried* was released, O'Brien visited another one of my classes, this one solely on the Vietnam War. Also in attendance were the book editors from the *Saint Paul Pioneer Press* and the *Minneapolis Star Tribune*. O'Brien started out by saying that he would like to tell us something about himself back in 1968. He admitted that what he was about to tell us embarrassed him, and that he had never told it to anyone before. He told us he was from Worthington, Minnesota, and that he had graduated from Macalester College in St. Paul. He related that when he was drafted in the summer of 1968, he worked in the Armour meatpacking plant, where his job was to remove blood clots from the necks of dead pigs. He mentioned that it was impossible to get rid of the pig smell and that he therefore had trouble getting dates. He talked at length about his misgivings regarding the morality of the war. During this narration—and with increasing enthusiasm as it went on for some twenty minutes—one of the reviewers was writing down all this fantastically good copy. Eventually, O'Brien told us that because of his opposition to the war, in desperation he headed north—to the Tip Top Lodge on the Rainy River. He ended his "confession" by saying, "I passed through towns with familiar names, through the pine forests and down to the prairie, and then to Vietnam. . . . I was a coward. I went to war."

There was an electric silence in the classroom. Everyone was spellbound by the personal details O'Brien had shared with them and by his honesty. Whereupon he said, "There are two things you should know about what I just told you: all of it is made up, and all of it is absolutely true." When the reviewer from one of the papers heard "All of it is made up," he immediately began feverishly erasing everything he had written down. After all, he couldn't print lies. There's got to be more than a mere dotted line between fiction and reality. He simply could not allow "all made up" and "all absolutely true" to coexist. You have to be on one side of the border or the other. I think he left the classroom that day in "a new confusion of his understanding."

Moving chronologically through O'Brien's three Vietnam books, we can notice the metamorphosis of a solid line to a dotted line to one that sometimes disappears altogether. In part we witness these metamorphoses in the changing role of O'Brien himself in his three books. We first find him playing himself, in memoir fashion [in *If I Die in A Combat Zone*]. Then he creates the artistic-minded O'Brien persona in Paul Berlin [in *Going After Cacciato*]. Finally, in an act of aesthetic and epistemological audacity, he creates a character named Tim O'Brien who isn't Tim O'Brien [in *The Things They Carried*].... In an interview with [American writer] Michael Coffey, O'Brien states: "All along, I knew I wanted to have a book in which my name, Tim, appeared even though Tim would not be me; that's all I knew." Why would O'Brien want to do this? And what are the implications of such a decision?

To answer the second question first, O'Brien seems to accept as his starting point the fictionality of *all* thought. Furthermore, the more conscious we are of fictionality, the greater the likelihood of grasping some small part of reality. Facts, by themselves, so he tells us in *Cacciato*, simply don't add up to anything much. In the Coffey interview, he says "... of the whole time I spent there [Vietnam] I remember maybe a week's worth of stuff."

Regarding the first question, if all thought is fictional, that includes the way we think of ourselves. To think of the real self as a single, fixed, objective, finished entity is as inappropriate as stopping the motion of a mobile, then believing we haven't radically altered its essence. Bluntly, Tim is not Tim because as author he is not God. Not ever able to know his self directly and absolutely, he too must be mediated [indirectly represented] by a persona. Another plausible explanation for O'Brien's decision to make Tim not Tim is that, fortunately, he couldn't forget Doc Peret's fifteen-year-old advice [in *Going After Cacciato*: "observation requires inward-looking, a study of the very machinery of observation—the mirrors and filters and wiring and circuits of the observing instrument"]. As a work of metafiction, *Carried* looks at the components of the "observing instrument" itself. Simply translated, the metaphor means we must study the way all reality is mediated by how, where, and when we look at it. O'Brien knows that reality is accessible *only* through mediation. That being the case, he spurns the Western paradigm of Manichaean dualism [that opposites are separate from and unrelated to each other], which convinces most of the people most of the time that they can tell the difference between reality and fiction. *Carried*, on the other hand, seems to be written on the assumption that there is only conscious and unconscious fiction, conscious and unconscious paradigms. Thus, O'Brien has fictional status both as character and author. So, instead of pretending to be real, O'Brien really pretends. As such, his metafiction writes a contract between reader and fiction that is similar to the one between audience and the theatre that operates with the being of real pretense, as opposed to the pretense of being real.

The Things They Carried Is a War Story About Writing War Stories

Catherine Calloway

Catherine Calloway is a professor and the director of graduate studies in English at Arkansas State University–Jonesboro. She has written a number of articles on Vietnam War literature.

Catherine Calloway views The Things They Carried *as an example of metafiction, a type of writing in which the author consciously draws the reader's attention to the artificial quality of the story he or she is crafting; the aim is to pose questions about the nature of fiction and reality. In its form as well as its content, Calloway suggests,* The Things They Carried *is hard to pin down and poses more questions than it answers: Is it a novel or a group of related stories? Are the characters real or imagined? Is it a work of fiction or nonfiction? Calloway maintains that the ambiguity driving such questions is intentional. Just as the war itself was ambiguous and confusing, so too is O'Brien's form and content. O'Brien uses the power of the imagination to craft a powerful story, and while there are no easy answers as to why wars are fought and what they mean, the best a writer can do is to keep the stories alive.*

*T*he Things They Carried begins with a litany of items that the soldiers "hump" [carry] in the Vietnam War—assorted weapons, dog tags, flak jackets, ear plugs, cigarettes, insect repellent, letters, can openers, C-rations [packaged, prepared meals], jungle boots, maps, medical supplies, and explosives as well as memories, reputations, and personal histories. In addi-

Catherine Calloway, "'How to Tell a True War Story': Metafiction in *The Things They Carried.*" *Critique: Studies in Contemporary Fiction* 36, June 1995. Reprinted by permission.

tion, the reader soon learns, the soldiers also carry stories: stories that connect "the past to the future," stories that can "make the dead talk," stories that "never seem . . . to end," stories that are "beyond telling," and stories "that swirl back and forth across the border between trivia and bedlam, the mad and the mundane." Although perhaps few of the stories in *The Things They Carried* are as brief as the well-known Vietnam War tale related by [American author] Michael Herr in *Dispatches*—"'Patrol went up the mountain. One man came back. He died before he could tell us what happened'"—many are in their own way as enigmatic. The tales included in O'Brien's twenty-two chapters range from several lines to many pages and demonstrate well the impossibility of knowing the reality of the war in absolute terms. Sometimes stories are abandoned, only to be continued pages or chapters later. At other times, the narrator begins to tell a story, only to have another character finish the tale. Still other stories are told as if true accounts, only for their validity to be immediately questioned or denied. O'Brien draws the reader into the text, calling the reader's attention to the process of invention and challenging him to determine which, if any, of the stories are true. As a result, the stories become epistemological [having to do with the study of knowledge] tools, multidimensional windows through which the war, the world, and the ways of telling a war story can be viewed from many different angles and visions.

The Difficulty of Knowing

The epistemological ambivalence of the stories in *The Things They Carried* is reinforced by the book's ambiguity of style and structure. What exactly is *The Things They Carried* in terms of technique? Many reviewers refer to the work as a series of short stories, but it is much more than that. *The Things They Carried* is a combat novel, yet it is not a combat novel. It is also a blend of traditional and untraditional forms—a collection, [journalist] Gene Lyons says, of "short stories, essays, anecdotes, narrative fragments, jokes, fables, biographical and autobiographical sketches, and philosophical asides." It has been called both "a unified narrative with chapters that stand perfectly on their own" [by writer Michael Coffey] and a series of "22 discontinuous sections" [by critic and writer Bruce Bawer].

Also ambiguous is the issue of how much of the book is autobiography. The relationship between fiction and reality arises early in the text when the reader learns the first of many parallels that emerge as the book progresses: that the protagonist and narrator, like the real author of *The Things They Carried*, is named Tim O'Brien. Both the real and the fictional Tim O'Brien are in their forties and are natives of Minnesota, writers who graduated Phi Beta Kappa from Macalester College [in Minnesota], served as grunts in Vietnam after having been drafted at age twenty-one, attended graduate school at Harvard University, and wrote books entitled *If I Die in a Combat Zone* and *Going After Cacciato*. Other events of the protagonist's life are apparently invention. Unlike the real Tim O'Brien, the protagonist has a nine-year-old daughter named Kathleen and makes a return journey to Vietnam years after the war is over.[1] However, even the other supposedly fictional characters of the book sound real because of an epigraph preceding the stories that states, "This book is lovingly dedicated to the men of Alpha Company, and in particular to Jimmy Cross, Norman Bowker, Rat Kiley, Mitchell Sanders, Henry Dobbins, and Kiowa," leading the reader to wonder if the men of Alpha Company are real or imaginary.

Clearly O'Brien resists a simplistic classification of his latest work. In both the preface to the book and in an interview with [*Los Angeles Times* reporter] Elizabeth Mehren, he terms *The Things They Carried* "'fiction . . . a novel,'" but in an interview with [author] Martin Naparsteck, he refers to the work

---

1. The real O'Brien did return to Vietnam in 1994.

as a "sort of half novel, half group of stories. It's part nonfiction, too," he insists. And, as Naparsteck points out, the work "resists easy categorization: it is part novel, part collection of stories, part essays, part journalism; it is, more significantly, all at the same time."

As O'Brien's extensive focus on storytelling indicates, *The Things They Carried* is also a work of contemporary metafiction, what [literary theorist] Robert Scholes first termed fabulation or "ethically controlled fantasy." According to [literary critic] Patricia Waugh,

> Metafiction is a term given to fictional writing which self-consciously and systematically draws attention to its status as an artefact in order to pose questions about the relationship between fiction and reality. In providing a critique of their own methods of construction, such writings not only examine the fundamental structures of narrative fiction, they also explore the possible fictionality of the world outside the literary fictional text.

A Book About Writing Books

Like O'Brien's earlier novel, the critically acclaimed *Going After Cacciato*, *The Things They Carried* considers the process of writing; it is, in fact, as much about the process of writing as it is the text of a literary work. By examining imagination and memory, two main components that O'Brien feels are important to a writer of fiction, and by providing so many layers of technique in one work, O'Brien delves into the origins of fictional creation. In focusing so extensively on what a war story is or is not, O'Brien writes a war story as he examines the process of writing one. To echo what [literary critic] Philip Beidler has stated about *Going After Cacciato*, "the form" of *The Things They Carried* thus becomes "its content"; the medium becomes the message.

"I'm forty-three years old, and a writer now," O'Brien's protagonist states periodically throughout the book, directly referring to his role as author and to the status of his work as artifice. "Much of it [the war] is hard to remember," he comments. "I sit at this typewriter and stare through my words and watch Kiowa sinking into the deep muck of a shit field, or Curt Lemon hanging in pieces from a tree, and as I write about these things, the remembering is turned into a kind of rehappening." The "rehappening" takes the form of a number of types of stories: some happy, some sad, some peaceful, some bloody, some wacky. We learn of Ted Lavender, who is "zapped [shot] while zipping" after urinating, of the paranoid friendship of Dave Jensen and Lee Strunk, of the revenge plot against Bobby Jorgenson, an unskilled medic who almost accidentally kills the narrator, of the moral confusion of the protagonist who fishes on the Rainy River and dreams of desertion to Canada, and Mary Ann Bell, Mark Fossie's blue-eyed, blonde, seventeen-year-old girlfriend, who is chillingly attracted to life in a combat zone.

Some stories only indirectly reflect the process of writing; other selections include obvious metafictional devices. In certain sections of the book, entire chapters are devoted to discussing form and technique. A good example is "Notes," which elaborates on "Speaking of Courage," the story that precedes it. The serious reader of the real Tim O'Brien's fiction recognizes "Speaking of Courage" as having first been published in the Summer 1976 issue of *Massachusetts Review*. This earlier version of the story plays off chapter 14 of *Going After Cacciato*, "Upon Almost Winning the Silver Star," in which the protagonist, Paul Berlin, is thinking about how he might have won the Silver Star for bravery in Vietnam had he had the courage to rescue Frenchie Tucker, a character shot while searching a tunnel. However, in *The Things They Carried*'s version of "Speaking of Courage," the protagonist is not Paul Berlin, but Norman Bowker, who wishes he had had the courage to save Kiowa, a soldier who dies in a field of excrement during a mortar attack. Such shifts in character and events tempt the reader into textual participation, leading him to question the ambiguous nature of reality. Who really did not win the Silver Star for bravery? Paul Berlin, Norman Bowker, or Tim O'Brien? Who actually needed saving? Frenchie Tucker or Kiowa? Which version of the story, if either, is accurate? The inclusion of a metafictional chapter presenting the background behind the tale provides no definite answers or resolutions. We learn that Norman Bowker, who eventually commits suicide, asks the narrator to compose the story and that the author has revised the tale for inclusion in *The Things They Carried* because a postwar story is more appropriate for the later book than for *Going After Cacciato*. However, O'Brien's admission that much of the story is still invention compels the reader to wonder about the truth. The narrator assures us that the truth is that "Norman did not experience a failure of nerve that night . . . or lose the Silver Star for valor." Can even this version be believed? Was there really a Norman Bowker, or is he, too, only fictional?

Fiction and Reality

Even more significant, the reader is led to question the reality of many, if not all, of the stories in the book. The narrator insists that the story of Curt Lemon's death, for instance, is "all exactly true" then states eight pages later that he has told Curt's story previously—"many times, many versions"—before narrating yet another version. As a result, any and all accounts of the incident are questionable. Similarly, the reader is led to doubt the validity of many of the tales told by other characters in the book. The narrator remarks that Rat Kiley's stories, such as the one about Mary Ann Bell in "Sweetheart of the Song Tra Bong," are particularly ambiguous:

> For Rat Kiley . . . facts were formed by sensation, not the other way around, and when you listened to one of his stories, you'd find yourself performing rapid calculations in

Tim O'Brien begins his novel The Things They Carried *with a list of objects the Vietnam soldiers carried: weapons, dog tags, cigarettes, etc. The soldiers also bore their stories and emotions.* Photo by Ian Brodie/Express/Getty Images.

your head, subtracting superlatives, figuring the square root of an absolute and then multiplying by maybe.

Still other characters admit the fictionality of their stories. Mitchell Sanders, in the ironically titled "How to Tell a True War Story," confesses to the protagonist that although his tale is the truth, parts of it are pure invention. "'Last night, man,'" Sanders states, "'I had to make up a few things . . . The glee club. There wasn't any glee club . . . No opera,'" either. "'But,'" he adds, "'it's still true.'"

O'Brien shares the criteria with which the writer or teller and the reader or listener must be concerned by giving an extended definition of what a war story is or is not. The chapter "How to Tell a True War Story" focuses most extensively on the features that might be found in a "true" war tale. "A true war story is never moral," the narrator states. "It does not instruct, nor encourage virtue, nor suggest models of proper human behavior, nor restrain men from doing the things men have always done." Furthermore, a true war story has an "absolute and uncompromising allegiance to obscenity and evil," is embarrassing, may not be believable, seems to go on forever, does "not generalize" or "indulge in abstraction or analysis," does not necessarily make "a point," and sometimes cannot even be told. True war stories, the reader soon realizes, are like the nature of the Vietnam War itself; "the only certainty is overwhelming ambiguity." "The final and definitive truth" cannot be derived, and any "truths are contradictory."

By defining a war story so broadly, O'Brien writes more stories, interspersing the definitions with examples from the war to illustrate them. What is particularly significant about the examples is that they are given in segments, a technique that actively engages the readers in the process of textual creation. Characters who are mentioned as having died early in the work are brought back to life through flashbacks in other parts of the text so that we can see who these characters are, what they are like, and how they die. For instance, in the story, "Spin," the narrator first refers to the death of Curt Lemon, a soldier blown apart by a booby trap, but the reader does not learn the details of the tragedy until four stories later in "How to Tell a True War Story." Even then, the reader must piece together the details of Curt's death throughout that particular tale. The first reference to Lemon appears on the third page of the story when O'Brien matter-of-factly states, "The dead guy's name was Curt Lemon." Lemon's death is briefly mentioned a few paragraphs later, but additional details surrounding the incident are not given at once but are revealed gradually throughout the story, in between digressive stories narrated by two other soldiers, Rat Kiley and Mitchell Sanders. Each fragment about Curt's accident illustrates the situation more graphically. Near the beginning of the tale, O'Brien describes the death somewhat poetically. Curt is "a handsome kid, really. Sharp grey eyes, lean and narrow-waisted, and when he died it was almost beautiful, the way the sunlight came around him and lifted him up and sucked him high into a tree full of moss and vines and white blossoms." Lemon is not mentioned again for seven pages, at which time O'Brien illustrates the effect of Lemon's death upon the other soldiers by detailing how Rat Kiley, avenging Curt's death, mutilates and kills a baby water buffalo. When later in the story Lemon's accident is narrated for the third time, the reader is finally told what was briefly alluded to in the earlier tale "Spin": how the soldiers had to peel Curt Lemon's body parts from a tree.

The story of Curt Lemon does not end with "How to Tell a True War Story" but is narrated further in two other stories, "The Dentist" and "The Lives of the Dead." In "The Lives of the Dead," for example, Curt is resurrected through a story of his trick-or-treating in Vietnamese hootches on Halloween for whatever goodies he can get: "candles and joss sticks and a pair of black pajamas and statuettes of the smiling Buddha." To hear Rat Kiley tell it, the narrator comments, "you'd never know that Curt Lemon was dead. He was still out there in the dark, naked and painted up, trick-or-treating, sliding from hootch to hootch in that crazy white ghost mask." To further complicate matters, in "The Lives of the Dead," O'Brien alludes to a soldier other than Curt, Stink Harris, from a previous literary work, *Going After Cacciato*, written over a decade before *The Things They Carried*. Thus, the epistemological uncertainty in the stories is mirrored by the fact that O'Brien presents events that take place in a fragmented form rather than in a straightforward, linear fashion. The reader has to piece together information, such as the circumstances surrounding the characters' deaths, in the same manner that the characters must piece together the reality of the war, or, for that matter, Curt Lemon's body.

The Issue of Truth

The issue of truth is particularly a main crux of the events surrounding "The Man I Killed," a story that O'Brien places near the center of the book. Gradually interspersed throughout the stories that make up *The Things They Carried* are references to a Vietnamese soldier, "A slim, dead, dainty young man of about twenty" with "a star-shaped hole" in his face, who is first mentioned in the story "Spin" and whose death still haunts the narrator long after the end of the war. Nine chapters after "Spin," in "The Man I Killed," the protagonist graphically describes the dead Vietnamese youth as well as creates a personal history for him; he envisions the young man to have been a reluctant soldier who hated violence and "loved mathematics," a university-educated man who "had been a soldier for only a single day" and who, like the narrator, perhaps went to war only to avoid "disgracing himself, and therefore his family and village." "Ambush," the story immediately following "The Man I Killed," provides yet another kaleidoscopic fictional frame of the incident, describing in detail the events that lead up to the narrator's killing of the young soldier and ending with a version of the event that suggests that the young man does not die at all. The reader is forced to connect the threads of the story in between several chapters that span over a hundred pages; not until a later chapter, "Good Form," where the protagonist narrates three more stories of the event, does the reader fully question the truth of the incident. In the first version in "Good Form," the narrator reverses the details of the earlier stories and denies that he was the thrower of the grenade that killed the man. "Twenty years ago I watched a man die on a trail near the village of My Khe," he states. "I did not kill him. But I was present, you see, and my presence was guilt enough." However, he immediately admits that "Even that story is made up" and tells instead what he terms "the happening-truth":

> I was once a soldier. There were many bodies, real bodies with real faces, but I was young then and I was afraid to look. And now, twenty years later, I'm left with faceless responsibility and faceless grief.

In still a third version, "the happening-truth" is replaced with "the story-truth." According to the protagonist, the Vietnamese soldier

> was a slim, dead, almost dainty young man of about twenty. He lay in the center of a red clay trail near the village of My Khe. His jaw was in his throat. His one eye was shut, the other eye was a star-shaped hole. I killed him.

But the reader wonders, did the narrator kill the young man? When the narrator's nine-year-old daughter demands, "'Daddy, tell the truth . . . did you ever kill anybody,'" the narrator reveals that he "can say, honestly, 'Of course not,'" or he "can say, honestly, 'Yes.'"

The Miracle of Vision

According to [Danish poet] Inger Christensen, one of the most important elements of metafiction is "the novelist's message." At least one reviewer has reduced O'Brien's message in *The Things They Carried* to the moral "'Death sucks'"; the book, however, reveals an even greater thematic concern. "Stories can save us," asserts the protagonist in "The Lives of the Dead," the concluding story of the text, where fiction is used as a means of resurrecting the deceased. In this multiple narrative, O'Brien juxtaposes tales of death in Vietnam with an account of the death of Linda, a nine-year-old girl who had a brain tumor. As the protagonist tells Linda's story, he also comments on the nature and power of fiction. Stories, he writes, are "a kind of dreaming, [where] the dead sometimes smile and sit up and return to the world." The narrator of "The Lives of the Dead" thus seeks to keep his own friends alive through the art of storytelling. "As a writer now," he asserts,

> I want to save Linda's life. Not her body—her life . . . in a story I can steal her soul. I can revive, at least briefly, that which is absolute and unchanging. . . . In a story, miracles

can happen. Linda can smile and sit up. She can reach out, touch my wrist, and say, "Timmy, stop crying."

Past, present, and future merge into one story as through fiction O'Brien zips "across the surface of . . . [his] own history, moving fast, riding the melt beneath the blades, doing loops and spins . . . as Tim trying to save Timmy's life with a story." His story mirrors his own creative image of history, "a blade tracing loops on ice," as his metafictive narrative circles on three levels: the war of a little boy's soul as he tries to understand the death of a friend, the Vietnam War of a twenty-three-year-old infantry sergeant, and the war of "guilt and sorrow" faced by "a middle-aged writer" who must deal with the past.

In focusing so extensively on the power of fiction and on what a war story is or is not in *The Things They Carried*, O'Brien writes a multidimensional war story even as he examines the process of writing one. His tales become stories within stories or multilayered texts within texts within texts. The book's genius is a seeming inevitability of form that perfectly embodies its theme—the miracle of vision—the eternally protean and volatile capacity of the imagination, which may invent that which it has the will and vision to conceive. "In the end," the narrator states,

> a true war story is never about war. It's about sunlight. It's about the special way that dawn spreads out on a river when you know you must cross the river and march into the mountains and do things you are afraid to do. It's about love and memory. It's about sorrow. It's about sisters who never write back and people who never listen.

How, then, can a true war story be told? Perhaps the best way, O'Brien says, is to "just keep on telling it."

O'Brien Uses Storytelling to Ease the Trauma of War

Mark Heberle

Mark Heberle has served as a professor of English at the University of Hawaii at Manoa. His books include Thirty Years After: New Essays on Vietnam War, Literature, Film, and Art.

In this selection, Mark Heberle examines the final story of The Things They Carried, *titled "The Lives of the Dead," from a psychological viewpoint, exploring the notion of trauma, not only in war but also in life in general. He suggests that at the conclusion of the book, O'Brien brings back those who have died by using storytelling and memory. According to Heberle, in combining accounts of his deceased fellow soldiers and his childhood girlfriend who died at age nine, O'Brien transcends the war. In resurrecting these lives, the persona known as "Tim O'Brien" in the story confronts the traumatic experiences of his life, translating into fiction the real-life anguish he could not bear.*

*T*he Things They Carried ends with "The Lives of the Dead," an account of how the narrator became a professional writer. Although published as an independent story in the January 1989 issue of [the men's magazine] *Esquire*, the piece is a deliberate conclusion to the book, incorporating and dramatizing once more what [*The Things They Carried*] has exemplified about true war stories and their relationship to traumatic experiences. Beginning with the simple assertion that "stories can save us," this final fiction resurrects [characters who died in previous stories:] Ted Lavender, Kiowa, Curt Lemon, "an old man sprawled beside a pigpen, and several others whose bodies I once lifted and dumped into a truck.

Mark Heberle, "Chapter 6: True War Stories," *A Trauma Artist: Tim O'Brien and the Fiction of Vietnam*, University of Iowa Press, 2001, pp. 211–15. Reprinted by permission.

They're all dead. But in a story," the narrator's introduction continues, "the dead sometimes smile and sit up and return to the world." Combining the tropes [literary devices] of memory and storytelling, "Lives" brings back the war dead in brief episodes that alternate with the narrator's account of his love for his grade-school classmate Linda, their first and only date, her death from brain cancer at the age of nine, and his dreaming her alive thereafter. By combining Vietnam and a love story, soldiers and nine-year-olds, "The Lives of the Dead" transcends the war and exemplifies the narrator's earlier insistence that "a true war story is never about war."

A Story Filled with Corpses

The paradox of the title identifies its real subject, a central concern of O'Brien's fifth book as a whole: the ways survivors carry the dead with them through the rest of their lives. "The Lives of the Dead" is filled with descriptions of corpses: an old Vietnamese farmer killed by an American air strike on an unfriendly village; Ted Lavender; *The Man Who Never Was*, a dead body dropped along the French coast to deceive the Nazis about the D-Day [June 6, 1944; the first day of the Allied invasion of occupied Europe] landings in a movie that Timmy and Linda saw on their one date; Linda's body in her funeral home casket, "bloated," the skin "at her cheeks ... stretched out tight like the rubber skin on a balloon just before it pops open"; twenty-seven "enemy KIAs" [soldiers killed in action] dumped into a truck by Tim O'Brien and Mitchell Sanders after their battle in the mountains—all "badly bloated ... clothing ... stretched tight like sausage skins ... heavy ... feet ... bluish green and cold." For Timmy, however, "It didn't seem real. A mistake, I thought. The girl lying in the white casket wasn't Linda.... I knew this was Linda, but even so I couldn't find much to recognize.... She looked dead. She looked heavy and totally dead." And for Mitchell Sanders, gathering the remains of a great victory that he and the narrator have survived brings a comparably banal enlightenment:

> At one point [he] looked at me and said, "Hey, man, I just realized something."

> "What?"

> He wiped his eyes and spoke very quietly, as if awed by his own wisdom.

> "Death sucks," he said.

The human imagination is unsatisfied with this trite truth, as Timmy's bewilderment and Sanders's tears for the enemy suggest, and O'Brien dramatizes various attempts to supplement or transmute the dead body throughout the story. "The Lives of the Dead" begins with a traumatic experience for the narrator, who cannot look at the decaying corpse of the old man who is "the only confirmed kill" of Jimmy Cross's punitive air strike. A newcomer to the war, he is further appalled as his comrades shake the corpse's hand and then prop it up as the guest of honor at a macabre get-acquainted party that gradually turns "that awesome act of greeting the dead" into a ceremony: "They proposed toasts. They lifted their canteens and drank to the old man's family and ancestors, his many grandchildren, his newfound life after death. It was more than mockery. There was a formality to it, like a funeral without the sadness." Kiowa comforts him later in the day, praising the courage of the narrator's refusal to participate, wishing that he had done the same but also reassuring him that "you're new here. You'll get used to it," since he assumes that "this was your first look at a real body." The necrology [obituary] of the scene is not simply repulsive, however, as the narrator realizes. Underneath the GIs' ghoulish humor and postmortem sadism lies an unconscious awareness of the mortality that they share with the Vietnamese farmer and an attempt to imagine beyond it. In "Night Life," the previous piece in *Things*, Rat Kiley has a nervous breakdown when he begins to see himself and his comrades as potential corpses, imagining them as a collection of organic body parts rather than as human beings. By contrast, here the narrator's comrades transform a corpse into a life to be celebrated beyond the "real body." Their grotesquerie contrasts strikingly with the sterile funeral home where Timmy is left bewildered and unsatisfied by the reality of Linda's preserved body.

The Resurrection of the Dead

The resurrection of the dead pervades O'Brien's final work. Kiowa comes back here, after all, as the comforter at the end of this first episode. *Things* began with Ted Lavender's death, and it ends with his corpse waiting for a medevac but miraculously reanimated as Mitchell Sanders and the rest of the platoon conduct a dialogue with their comrade before sending him home: "'There it is, my man, this chopper gonna take you up high and cool. Gonna relax you. Gonna alter your whole perspective on this sorry, sorry shit.' ... 'Roger that,' somebody said. 'I'm ready to fly.'" The last we hear and see of Rat Kiley's dearest friend [Curt Lemon] is not the obliteration of his body but the full account of his trick-or-treating in the Vietnamese countryside on Halloween, "almost stark naked, the story went, just boots and balls and an M-16. . . . To listen to the story, especially as Rat Kiley told it, you'd never know that Curt Lemon was dead. He was still out there in the dark, naked and painted up, trick-or-treating, sliding from hootch [hut] to hootch in that crazy white ghost mask."

It is the resurrection of Linda, however, that has made all the others possible. Although Kiowa assumes that the Vietnamese farmer provides Tim O'Brien's first look at a corpse, he is wrong. "It sounds funny," O'Brien's persona tells him, "but that poor old man, he reminds me of . . . I mean, there's this girl I used to know. I took her to the movies once. My first date." "[T]hat's a bad date," Kiowa understandably responds, ending the first section of "The Lives of the Dead." Most of the rest is taken up with the narrator's memories of his love for Linda, their going off to see *The Man Who Never Was* with his parents as chaperones, the exposure of her fatal illness, her death, and his visit to the funeral home. As he recounts it, his life as a storyteller began when he imagined his love alive the day after Linda died, in "a pink dress and shiny black shoes," all traces of her illness gone, "laughing and running up the empty street, kicking a big aluminum water bucket." Timmy breaks down, knowing that she's dead, but Linda insists that "it doesn't *matter*" and forces him to stop crying. Thereafter, Linda's death and his grief are replaced by dreaming her back to life and his subsequent career as an author: "She was dead. I understood that. After all, I'd seen her body, and yet even as a nine-year-old I had begun to practice the magic of stories. Some I just dreamed up. Others I wrote down—the scenes and dialogue. And at nighttime I'd slide into sleep knowing that Linda would be there waiting for me. Once, I remember, we went ice skating late at night, tracing loops and circles under yellow floodlights." By asking what it's like to be dead, Timmy initially questions the truth of his own imagination, but Linda sets him straight: "'Well, right now,' she said, 'I'm *not* dead. But when I am, it's like ... I don't know, I guess it's like being inside a book that nobody's reading.'"

Saving Lives

According to this account, therefore, writing grows directly out of trauma but refashions it beyond the unreality of death. Like the rest of the dead, Linda comes back to life through the narrator's stories, but so does he as he examines a photograph of himself as a nine-year-old:

> [T]here is no doubt that the Timmy smiling at the camera is the Tim I am now. ... The human life is all one thing, like a

> blade tracing loops on ice: a little kid, a twenty-three-year-old infantry sergeant, a middle-aged writer knowing guilt and sorrow.
>
> And as a writer now, I want to save Linda's life. Not her body—her life.

In saving her, therefore, he saves himself. Near the end of "The Lives of the Dead," however, we are reminded that while stories can save lives, what is saved is itself a fiction: "I'm forty-three years old, and a writer now, still dreaming Linda alive in exactly the same way. She's not the embodied Linda; she's mostly made up, with a new identity and a new name. . . . Her real name doesn't matter. She was nine years old. I loved her and then she died." The facts are less important than the truth that the story has compelled us to believe. Employing the tropes of memory and storytelling for the last time as the book comes to an end, O'Brien uses them together not to represent the fact of death—even the dead are fictions in a true war story—but to save the lives of Linda and his other characters forever: "And yet right here, in the spell of memory and imagination, I can still see her as if through ice, as if I'm gazing into some other world, a place where there are no brain tumors and no funeral homes, where there are no bodies at all. I can see Kiowa, too, and Ted Lavender and Curt Lemon, and sometimes I can even see Timmy skating with Linda under the yellow floodlights. I'm young and happy. I'll never die." Ultimately, of course, by making us believe in the man who never was, fiction can create people who will never die.

A Separate Peace Through Storytelling

O'Brien's great book has certainly done both, but it is O'Brien's persona, a fictional creation, not necessarily O'Brien himself, who seems to have saved his life through writing by the end of "The Lives of the Dead." A survivor of trauma who has translated what he could not carry into true war stories, Tim O'Brien resembles the author's other protagonists in passing through fear, guilt, and grief to achieve his own separate peace. The narrator's ability to memorialize a terrible war so masterfully makes *The Things They Carried* O'Brien's most accomplished fiction, and his persona's ostensible resolution of his personal trauma also makes it the most redemptive. Yet Tim O'Brien's sense of well-being in *The Things They Carried* is also a function of his narrow characterization. Except for the relationships with his daughter and Linda, he has no life outside of writing; in fact, everything he does, says, or remembers in the book becomes part of its storytelling. Trauma is endlessly recirculated through the tropes of memory and storytelling or explicitly fabricated in multiple versions, never experienced directly by the fictional protagonist as it is in the three previous novels [*Northern Lights, Going After Cacciato*, and *The Nuclear Age*]. Like *Things*, O'Brien's next book [*In the Lake of the Woods*] will be formidably metafictional, but its hero's inescapable, comprehensive, and endless traumatization will cost him his life, not enable him to save it.

O'Brien Writes His Way to Spiritual Redemption

Alex Vernon

Alex Vernon graduated from the United States Military Academy at West Point and served in the First Gulf War (the 1990–91 response to Iraq's invasion of Kuwait). He has taught American literature and writing at Hendrix College in Arkansas and is the author of the memoir Most Succinctly Bred.

In this viewpoint, Alex Vernon argues that The Things They Carried *is Tim O'Brien's attempt to find spiritual redemption after his brutal time in Vietnam. Vernon says that the book is modeled in part on seventeenth-century English writer John Bunyan's* Pilgrim's Progress, *a Christian quest to find salvation for the soul, and that numerous Christian symbols in O'Brien's book make this motif apparent. Vernon states that he does not mean to imply that O'Brien can literally save souls destroyed by war or resurrect the dead, but that the writer is a metaphorical healer, a shaman who can offer some solace in the face of a horrific past.*

*T*he Things They Carried repeatedly attests to the power of storytelling to transform events and to affirm a new kind of truth, one more spiritual than factual, while somehow in the process redeeming us and resurrecting the dead. Such language comes most strongly in "The Lives of the Dead," the book's final story. "But this too is true," O'Brien's story begins: "stories can save us. . . . [I]n a story, which is a kind of dreaming, the dead sometimes smile and sit up and return to the world." O'Brien's narrator Tim recalls conversations he had as a child with a dead friend, the nine-year-old Linda. He recalls

Alex Vernon, "Salvation, Storytelling, and Pilgrimage in *The Things They Carried*," in *Soldiers Once and Still: Ernest Hemingway, James Salter, & Tim O'Brien*, University of Iowa Press, 2004, pp. 223–28. Reprinted by permission.

a movie they saw, *The Man Who Never Was,* about a corpse used by the Allies in World War II for delivering false operational plans to deceive the Germans and win the war—about, in other words, a dead man whose death and figurative resurrection saved the world from the evils of Nazi Germany. He recalls the stories told and retold about the dead soldiers from Vietnam, stories always slightly different with each telling, often elaborated beyond the limits of factual, earthly truth yet true to the spirit of using language to keep the dead alive. "But in a story," Tim the narrator writes, "which is a kind of dreaming, the dead sometimes smile and sit up and return to the world." Such he calls a "miracle," and Tim tells these stories "trying to save Timmy's life with a story"—trying to save the child that he was, his preadult, innocent, prelapsarian [before the biblical fall of humankind] self.

A Journey Toward Spiritual Salvation

The message O'Brien imparts we have heard before. By faithfully retelling the story of Christ in its several variations, by allowing themselves to believe against all fact in his death and resurrection, Christians animate him and in the process save their prelapsarian souls. His, the maxim goes, is the greatest story ever told. O'Brien seems to want us to read *The Things They Carried* as a literary analogue of the New Testament. The infantry platoon is led by the lieutenant [Jimmy Cross] with the significant last name and initials [Cross and J.C. for Jesus Christ]. With stories commenting on each other and confusing the facts while achieving a greater truth, with two stories ("Spin" and "How to Tell a True War Story") composed of Psalmlike fragments, the book's episodic structure does not wander far from the structural spirit of the Bible—a structure Maggie Dunn and Ann Morris, in their study of the composite novel, call "the sacred composite." ... *The Things They Carried* offers a number of morals, primarily the conspicuous moral of the stories surrounding Kiowa's death: that every

John Bunyan, author of Pilgrim's Progress. *Alex Vernon believes O'Brien's novel* The Things They Carried *is partly modeled after Bunyan's book.* Library of Congress.

citizen, even the old man in Omaha who didn't vote, is responsible for the war and for everything in the war, from Kiowa's death to My Lai [the site of a massacre by American troops].

The opening and title story of *The Things They Carried* details the burdens, physical and emotional, carried by infantrymen in Vietnam. By immediately inviting the reader to join the characters in this journey, a journey that has moral dimensions and the potential for spiritual salvation, *The Things They Carried* echoes [seventeenth-century English religious writer John] Bunyan's *Pilgrim's Progress*. The very title of O'Brien's book and lead story strongly suggests the burden carried by Bunyan's [protagonist named] Christian—indeed, this may be the reason O'Brien selected this story as lead and title instead of, for example, "How to Tell a True War Story." [Literary scholar] Paul Fussell, whose *The Great War and Modern Memory* (1975) is a seminal work of literary and cultural criticism on the war, writes of a reference to Bunyan by a World War I *British Daily Express* columnist, that the troops overseas, "who had named one of the support trenches of the Hohenzollern Redoubt [a German fortification along the Western Front] 'Pilgrim's Progress,' . . . would not fail to notice the similarity between a fully loaded soldier, marching to and from the line with haversack, ground-sheet, blanket, rifle, and ammunition, and the image of Christian at the outset of his adventures." Likewise, O'Brien's soldiers at the very outset of their narrative adventure carry can openers, pocket knives, heat tabs [salt pills], C rations [prepackaged meals], water, steel helmets, boots, extra socks, flak jackets [that protect against shrapnel], bandages, ponchos, poncho liners, mosquito netting, machetes, and arms and ammunition.

Pilgrim's Progress and *The Things They Carried* Compared

Fussell traces a number of references and similarities in World War I British memoirs to Bunyan's parable and other less popular romance quests: the carried burdens, the ghostliness of the experience, the "action of moving physically through some terrible topographical nightmare," and the incalculable allusions to Bunyan's Slough of Despond and his Valley of the Shadow of Death [symbolic place names in *Pilgrim's Progress*]—all of which O'Brien's book re-creates, with twists. In this collection of stories patched together from previously published and new pieces, Christian isn't just the aptly named Jimmy Cross. He is also, and perhaps more directly, Tim on his narrative quest for salvation. The Slough of Despond, in which Christian finds himself mired in muck, becomes O'Brien's shit field. If the character [named] Help provides the helping hand that pulls Christian from the muck [in *Pilgrim's Progress*], Norman Bowker (or Tim the narrator?) fails to reach his hand out to save Kiowa—who always carries a New Testament and "had been raised to believe in the prom- ise of salvation under Jesus Christ"—from the sucking field of mud and shit. The disparate fates of Christian and Kiowa aside, Bunyan's and O'Brien's messages are startlingly similar: We are all responsible to one another, we are in this all too earthly life together. The ambiguity of [which character's] ac- tions led to Kiowa's death, and who failed to pull him out of the shit field, underscores the fact that one person isn't to blame. All are responsible.

Even the three stages of Christian's experience in Bun- yan—The Manner of his Setting Out, his Dangerous Journey, and his Safe Arrival at the Desired Country—work their way into O'Brien's structure which, though less linear, includes de- scriptions of Tim's prewar self and the manner of his submis- sion to the war, his wartime journey, and his postwar self's ar- rival home. That the fragmented and recursive [repetitious] nature of *The Things They Carried* has the linearity implied by a journey motif might not accord with many readers' experi- ence of reading the novel, as the novel certainly flirts with the suicidal repetition of Norman Bowker's self-destructive, Dan- tesque [after Dante Alighieri, author of the fourteenth-century classic *The Divine Comedy*] circling of the lake and his own veteran soul in "Speaking of Courage." Indeed, we can read the success of O'Brien's writing career through *The Things They Carried* and his 1994 novel *In the Lake of the Woods* and essay "The Vietnam in Me" as extended flirtations with this very dangerous, seductive world of his own memory. Depression and thoughts of suicide plague the author in "The Vietnam in Me," published after his first (and only) return trip to Vietnam twenty-five years after his tour of duty there, while at the end of *In the Lake of the Woods* the shades of Vietnam in [protagonist] John Wade's life create the situation that amounts to a kind of suicide when he is driven to get in his boat and motor out of the text and out of society permanently. Norman Bowker and his story very much belong to Tim O'Brien and his own narrative. Thus the question of whether *The Things They Carried*'s narrative journey delivers us—delivers Tim—to a place analogous to Christian's Celestial City, as Fussell finds World War I memoirs attempting to do, persists. The novel's recursive form signifies its status not as war story at all but as a postwar story of a veteran struggling with his demons.

Writing as a Ritualistic Act

I do not mean to suggest that O'Brien or Tim actually hopes to resurrect the dead or save lives destroyed by the war. The text's language of saving lives works metaphorically. Tim the narrator-character returns to war in his fiction desperately seeking some positive meaning in his own and his comrades' experiences. He wants to discover a way to alleviate his guilt and burden so that he can return to the war in his memory, emotionally survive the trip, and perhaps even gain from it. It had to mean *something*, didn't it? For all that suffering? He hopes to recover a little of his prewar innocence and his faith in himself, everyone else, and the future. He tries to create a religion of writing fiction as a means of transcending the horrible "happening-truth" of war. Even if writing affords only fleeting moments of transcendence, perhaps those moments can suffice to carry the soul along. The war itself offered him nothing but darkness; maybe, in writing about it, he can find a ray of light.

Writing for Tim the narrator thus becomes a ritual act, experienced as a dream state. Much of O'Brien's own aesthetic, in this novel and even more manifestly in [his earlier Vietnam novel] *Going After Cacciato*, also renders the narrator as in a dream state. [Scholar] Milton J. Bates finds *Cacciato* more akin to "the medieval dream-vision" than "either naturalism or 'magical realism'"—more akin to a work like Bunyan's. *The Things They Carried* is a dreamscape novel in its composition process and in Tim the character-narrator's mimicking of O'Brien the author's composition process. O'Brien's writing process is "a mixture of the subconscious and the directed . . .: I'm half living in a rational world and half living in a kind of trance, imagining." Tim the character-narrator submits himself to the same process in *Things*, as he describes one of his conversations with the dead Linda: "It was a kind of self-hypnosis. Partly willpower, partly faith, which is how stories arrive."

O'Brien's 1991 essay "The Magic Show" on the art of storytelling, published only a year after *Things*, connects this writing trance to the spiritual state in which the religious shaman operates, "watching the spirits beyond." The essay also explicitly connects O'Brien's artistic credo with the essential Christian one. The piece begins with the memory of his childhood hobby, magic. Its hold on him came from the sense of "the abiding mystery at its heart. Mystery everywhere— permeating mystery—even in the most ordinary objects of the world." Through magic he could imagine a universe "both infinite and inexplicable" where "anything was possible," where "the old rules were no longer binding," where, if he could restore an apparently cleaved necktie, he ought to be able to use his "wand to wake up the dead." O'Brien then reminds us of the dual role in many cultures of magician and storyteller, offices performed by the same person, most commonly in a religious context.

> The healer, or miracle worker, is also the teller of stories about prior miracles, or about miracles still to come. In Christianity, the personage of Jesus is presented as a doer of both earthly miracles and the ultimate heavenly miracle of salvation. At the same time Jesus is a teller of miraculous stories—the parables, for instance, or the larger story about damnation and redemption. The performance of miracles and the telling of stories become part of a whole. . . .

> The more I write and the more I dream, the more I accept this notion of the writer as a medium between two planes of being—the ordinary and the extraordinary—the embodied world of flesh, the disembodied world of idea and morality and spirit.

> In this sense, then, I must also believe that writing is essentially an act of faith. Faith in the heuristic [problem-solving or self-educating] power of the imagination. Faith in the fertility of the dream. Faith that as writers we might discover that which cannot be known through empirical means. (The notions of right and wrong, for instance. Good and evil. Ugliness and beauty.) Faith in story itself. Faith that story will lead, in some way, to epiphany or understanding or enlightenment.

The Writer as Shaman

The Things They Carried assigns this shamanistic role to Tim the narrator, who has preserved his childhood sweetheart Linda "in the spell of memory and imagination" in the same way he has preserved the soldiers he knew who died in Vietnam—and in the same way O'Brien writes, and for the same reasons: to happen onto epiphany or understanding or enlightenment; to transcend the ordinary and the actual, to work miracles, to find spiritual relief. Thus the actual Chip [a friend who appears in O'Brien's 1973 memoir *If I Die in a Combat Zone*] becomes the novel's Curt Lemon, whose death Tim reinvents for his own peace of mind:

> Twenty years later, I can still see the sunlight on Lemon's face. I can see him turning, looking back at Rat Kiley, then he laughed and took that curious half step from shade into sunlight, his face suddenly brown and shining, and when his foot touched down, in that instant, he must've thought it was the sunlight that was killing him. It was not the sunlight. It was a rigged 105 round [an artillery shell]. But if I could ever get the story right, how the sun seemed to gather around him and pick him up and lift him high into a tree, if I could somehow re-create the fatal whiteness of that light, the quick glare, the obvious cause and effect, then you would believe that the last thing Curt Lemon believed, which for him must've been the final truth.

In "The Lives of the Dead," Timmy, while dreaming, talks to the dead Linda, and in this same spirit of dreaming he reanimates his dead buddies. My point is that to read *The Things They Carried* as a journey or pilgrimage, we must read it not as a war story but as a postwar story, the story of the writer at his desk, not the soldier in the jungle, his childhood wand a pencil now, on an entirely different kind of journey.

Tim O'Brien Struggles with Guilt over the War

Tobey C. Herzog

Tobey C. Herzog has served as a professor of English at Wabash College in Indiana. His books include Vietnam War Stories: Innocence Lost *and* Writing Vietnam, Writing Life: Caputo, Heinemann, O'Brien, Butler.

In this viewpoint, Tobey C. Herzog explores the dual nature of the figure of Tim O'Brien in The Things They Carried. *O'Brien is both the book's author and one of its characters. The real O'Brien claims that the character is fictional, even though the two share numerous biographical similarities. According to Herzog, using a fictional persona with the same name allows the author to more effectively dramatize incidents and explore characters. One emotion shared by both Tim O'Briens is that of guilt— guilt about being too cowardly to resist the war, about killing the enemy, and about surviving the war when so many others did not. Herzog maintains that the persona Tim O'Brien seeks forgiveness, healing, and closure when he returns to Vietnam with his fictional daughter and buries a dead comrade's moccasins that he had kept for twenty years.*

A frequent point of confusion for readers of *The Things They Carried* is the fact that the names of the fictional author-narrator of this autobiography and the real author are identical; author O'Brien, however, notes that despite the same name and many of the same characteristics, "it [the narrator] isn't really me." Nevertheless, comparisons between the two O'Briens are inevitable, as are questions about how much of the material in this book is invented and how much is recalled by author O'Brien from his own life. Why did he use the same name? O'Brien responds to this question by describing a significant moment in his life and his writing career: "A month into the writing of the book [*Things*] . . . I found my name appearing." After about an hour of writing he began to feel the words and stories in his stomach and heart as a result of writing and reading his name in the manuscript. Such a magical intersecting of his writing life and real life became an important influence on this book and resulted in O'Brien's decision to continue using his name.

The Fictional Tim O'Brien

O'Brien has, however, used more than his own name in developing this fictional narrator's background and personality. Readers familiar with O'Brien's life will find several parallels between the lives of author and narrator, along with a few key differences. As revealed in the course of this fictional autobiography, the 43-year-old subject, who in 1989–1990 is the same age as O'Brien, lives in Massachusetts with a wife and daughter. He is a Vietnam veteran who has written about the war, specifically a novel called *Going After Cacciato* and an award-winning short story titled "Speaking of Courage." The fictional Tim grew up in Worthington, Minnesota; played shortstop in little league; graduated Phi Beta Kappa and summa cum laude from Macalaster College in 1968, where he was a [Eugene] McCarthy supporter in the presidential campaign; and soon after receiving a draft notice, reluctantly entered the army. He served his Vietnam tour in an area of operations just south of Chu Lai in Quang Ngai Province. During this time he was wounded twice. An "easy adjustment from war to peace" marked this Tim's return from the war and his enrollment in a graduate program at Harvard. So far the facts about this fictional character are strikingly similar to those in author O'Brien's life—except that he does not have a daughter and he was wounded only once. Furthermore, the views of the two O'Briens toward war and the citizens of Worthington are remarkably alike. At age 21, the fictional Tim believed the "American war in Vietnam seemed to me wrong. Certain blood was being shed for uncertain reasons." Also at this age, he condemned the ignorance of the adults in Worthington toward the war: "I held them personally and individually responsible—the polyestered Kiwanis boys. . . . They didn't know Bao Dai [the last reigning emperor of Vietnam, who stepped down in 1955] from the man in the moon. They didn't know history." Both of these quotes contain words author O'Brien has used in several interviews to comment on the same issues.

The question emerges whether author O'Brien's efforts at confusing the reader by including so many of these real facts from his life are more literary tricks? Or is the technique part of the overall message of the book about truth, literary lies, angles of perspective, storytelling, and the relationship between memory and imagination? The answer seems to be the latter; the method is the message illustrating the elusiveness of truth. As he does throughout this interconnected novel, frequently telling the same story from different perspectives and with different information, O'Brien seems to be exploring his own life from different angles that combine facts and invented details. The results are a heightened dramatic intensity to incidents, increased emotional responses from readers, and perhaps from O'Brien's point of view additional opportunities to explore possibilities for himself and his characters.

Exorcising Guilt

As the fictional Tim O'Brien presents the confessional thread of this autobiography, revealing his heart and mind, readers begin to understand that author O'Brien and narrator Tim O'Brien are also preoccupied with analogous issues—courage, embarrassment, cowardice, fear, death, revenge, guilt, and healing. Again, they face many of the same doubts, fears, emotions, and character changes that soldiers in all wars have confronted. Many of these moral, philosophical, and emotional topics first appeared in the nonfictional *If I Die* [*in a Combat Zone*] and reappear in the later works. In *The Things They Carried*, however, they are viewed from new angles and with much more story depth and emotional impact. For narrator Tim, and possibly author O'Brien, these confessions become an exorcising of guilt, a way to "relieve at least some of the pressure on my dreams." The narrator's moments of introspection also become emotional releases, opportunities to cut through the numbness that the war has created in him so he can feel again.

Perhaps the most dramatic confessional passages are those dealing with the narrator's guilt. Author-soldier O'Brien's guilt over his participation in the Vietnam War ("I was a coward"), described in *If I Die*, becomes narrator Tim's culpability over a similar decision to go to war. But this Tim's transgression also widens to include self-blame for the deaths of friends and foes and a sense of personal fault for the way the war has changed him. Although passages of autobiographical introspection appear throughout this novel, a few key stories focus exclusively on the narrator's examination of his memories, feelings, and this guilt—the things that 20 years after returning from Viet Nam "would never go away."

Some of this feeling of wrongdoing emerges from Tim's uneasiness about combat numbness to death and destruction, a condition to which many soldiers involuntarily succumb to stave off emotional collapse from viewing brutality on a daily basis. In Tim's case such dullness has remained with him years after the war: "There were times in my life when I couldn't feel much, not sadness or pity or passion, and somehow I blamed this place [Vietnam] for what I had become." Some of the narrator's confessions of sin involve another occurrence common among thoughtful individuals who confront the horrors of war—the frightening realization that during the war they have become very different people. As described in the story "Ghost Soldiers," Tim, who has undergone his own heart-of-darkness experience in war, is shocked that feelings of revenge and meanness inhabit the core of his character: "For all my education, all my fine liberal values, I now felt a deep coldness inside me, something dark and beyond reason. It's a hard thing to admit, even to myself, but I was capable of evil."

To Flee or Fight

Among these various forms of guilt to which Tim confesses, one of the most poignant and familiar emerges from the narrator's dilemma of whether to flee or fight, a recurring theme in O'Brien's works. As described in the short story "On the Rainy River," Tim O'Brien, like the real O'Brien, confronts this issue after his graduation from college. With a "draft notice tucked away in [his] wallet"—a similar line also appears in *If I Die*—the narrator spends six days at a fishing lodge on the Rainy River, which literally divides northern Minnesota from Canada and symbolically divides fighting from fleeing. The opportunity for a separate peace surfaces as Tim ponders escaping across the border into Canada. The competing arguments for and against flight raised in *If I Die* and *Going After Cacciato* reappear in this story, although they contain a dramatic intensity and depth of feeling missing in the earlier works: the argument of conscience—the war "seemed to me wrong"; the argument of personal safety—"for at the very center, was the raw fact of terror. I did not want to die"; the argument of society's censure—"I feared the war, yes, but I also feared exile"; and the argument of comfort and order—"all I wanted was to live the life I was born to—a mainstream life."

On the last day of his stay, Tim is taken fishing on the Rainy River by the lodge's 81-year-old proprietor, Elroy Berdahl, who as a quasi-father figure and confidant plays a role in this story similar to [the protagonist's commanding officer] Lieutenant Corson's in *Going After Cacciato* and [the protagonist's friend] Claude Rasmussen's in *In the Lake of the Woods.* Berdahl forces O'Brien to act when the old man takes the boat into Canadian territory and stops a short distance from land: "but I think he meant to bring me up against the realities, to guide me across the river and to take me to the edge and to stand a kind of vigil as I chose a life for myself." Like civilian O'Brien in *If I Die,* draftee O'Brien about to depart for Vietnam in the same book, and Paul Berlin, the fictional soldier [and protagonist of *Going After Cacciato*], this narrator Tim O'Brien must adjudicate competing personal values and choose a course of action. As his tears mix with hallucinations about fleeing to Canada or returning home, Tim, like his counterparts in the previous stories, decides to go to war.

Readers have read his rationale before in the previous war narratives: "I couldn't risk the embarrassment. . . . Even in my imagination . . . I couldn't make myself be brave." At this point the 43-year-old narrator condemns his earlier decision with words used previously in *If I Die* but with a conviction missing in that book: "I was a coward. I went to the war." With this judgment, Tim O'Brien the civilian, soldier, and author seems to merge with the fictional Tim O'Brien, but perhaps not with Paul Berlin—whose situation and character create a somewhat different angle on this dilemma.

Guilt over Killing

Another type of guilt, also borrowed from *If I Die,* surfaces in some of the introspective stories and commentaries as narrator Tim O'Brien broods over memories of battlefield deaths: "Here is the happening-truth. I was once a soldier. There were many bodies, real bodies with real faces, but I was young then and I was afraid to look. And now, twenty years later, I'm left with faceless responsibility and faceless grief." To explore this guilt, author O'Brien transforms his uneventful "Ambush" chapter in *If I Die* and another chapter from the same book titled "Mori," describing the death of a North Vietnamese Army nurse, into three very dramatic and personal sections within *The Things They Carried* titled "The Man I Killed," "Ambush," and "Good Form." In these chapters, Tim O'Brien examines his responsibility—direct as well as indirect—for the death of a Vietcong [Communist guerrillas in South Vietnam] soldier. Consistent with his pattern of mixing memory with imagination, fact with fiction, one detail with a conflicting detail, the narrator describes from different perspectives this soldier's death and Tim's subsequent remorse. In the first two stories, Tim recalls in detail a night ambush during which he killed the Vietnamese soldier. Years later still haunted by images of the body lying on the trail, the narrator confesses that "Even now I haven't finished sorting it out. Sometimes I forgive myself, other times I don't." But later in "Good Form," a commentary section, the 43-year-old narrator confesses something even more startling: He saw this enemy soldier die on a trail, but "I did not kill him. But I was present, you see, and my presence was guilt enough."

Survivor's Guilt

Such confessions of accountability for his actions or mere presence (the facts are left purposely vague) related to various deaths also lead to Tim's survival guilt. For instance, the recurring brief passages describing from various angles the death of fellow soldier Curt Lemon (Chip from *If I Die*) suggest such a self-censure, a typical reaction among soldiers. Moreover, in the section titled "The Lives of the Dead," the deaths of other squad members, of the Vietnamese soldier Tim did or did not kill, and of Vietnamese civilians merge with the death of nine-year-old Linda, Timmy's girlfriend in fourth grade. These fatalities across time and place link with each other and pierce the narrator's emotional numbness created by the war. In particular, memories of Linda's death resurrect Tim's feelings of intense loss, along with a form of survivor's guilt and embarrassment over his inability to be brave in standing up to a class bully taunting the young girl dying of a brain tumor.

The death that seems to haunt Tim the most, however, is Kiowa's gruesome demise in a shit field just outside a Vietnamese village. Once again mystery surrounds the death of this Bible-carrying Native American, who is one of Tim's best friends. As the event is described in "Speaking of Courage," readers wonder whether squad member Norman Bowker is responsible for the casualty (a failure to act) or whether, as suggested in "Notes," "In the Field," and "Field Trip," Tim is guilty of unintentional complicity in Kiowa's death (a similar failure to save the soldier). This contradiction of happening-truths is never resolved; the story-truth is, on the other hand, quite plain. At age 34 Tim returns with his daughter to Viet Nam and the site of Kiowa's death ("Field Trip"): "This little field, I thought, had swallowed so much. My best friend. My pride. My belief in myself as a man of small dignity and courage." In a scene somewhat reminiscent of Paul Perry's symbolic submersion in Pliney's Pond at the end of *Northern Lights*, Tim seeks forgiveness, closure, and healing for his war experiences by immersing himself in the river bordering the shit field and burying in the river bottom Kiowa's moccasins, which Tim has kept for 20 years: "Twenty years. A lot like yesterday, a lot like never. In a way, maybe, I'd gone under with Kiowa, and now after two decades I'd finally worked my way out."

The Things They Carried Presents a Complicated View of Gender

Susan Farrell

Susan Farrell has taught English at the College of Charleston. She is the author of Critical Companion to Kurt Vonnegut *and* Critical Companion to Tim O'Brien.

Because the first story of The Things They Carried *is so factual, writes Susan Farrell, readers tend to see the entire narrative thread of Lieutenant Jimmy Cross's tale as ironclad truth. But Cross is a romantic, Farrell insists, and his attempt to attribute the death of soldier Ted Lavender to his own sloppy leadership is unrealistic, as is his fantasy of his girlfriend, Martha, as pure and innocent. Cross's reaction to Lavender's death is to refashion himself as a man's man in the style of Western film actor John Wayne. But O'Brien, Farrell states, is not writing a tale to renounce the feminine in fighting men by pinning Lavender's death on Cross's schoolboy crush. O'Brien's depiction of gender during wartime proves more complicated than that. For example, the second story of the volume, "Love," portrays Martha as a strong, independent woman who perhaps has her own cross to bear.*

The book's opening story, "The Things They Carried," offers two competing narratives: the ultra-realistic, precise details of what the men carry (down to brand names and weights of objects listed in ounces) versus the more personal, more traumatic story of the death of Ted Lavender. Such a form underscores one of the novel's main concerns, the relation between fact and fiction—already a troubled question be-

Susan Farrell, "Tim O'Brien and Gender: A Defense of *The Things They Carried.*" *CEA Critic* 66-1, Fall 2003, pp. 1–21. Reprinted with permission.

fore the first story even begins. While the copyright page makes the usual disclaimers about this being an imaginative work of fiction, the book is dedicated to its characters, as if these are real people, and the epigraph from [Union soldier and prisoner-of-war] John Ransom's [Civil War memoir] *Andersonville Diary* asserts the truth of what is to follow. The concrete specificity of the lists in the opening story work along with the book's dedication and epigraph to set readers up to expect a hard-nosed, factual account of the war. Thus, we might mistakenly read Jimmy Cross's story as fact as well—an omniscient, third-person account of the reality of war experience. Such a reading would be a mistake, though. We must remember that the story of Ted Lavender's death is filtered through the subjective experience of Lieutenant Jimmy Cross. It is a narrative that increasingly interrupts and sub-sumes [takes over] the more objective story of the items the men carry with them in the field. Yet, it is *not* a story about men at war having to renounce the feminine. Rather, it is about the inevitable guilt associated with war deaths and what soldiers do with that guilt.

The Irrationality of Guilt

While Jimmy Cross certainly views Martha as inhabiting another world, separate from the war, and thus as representing home, purity, an innocence he no longer retains, I'd argue that readers are not supposed to make the same easy gender classifications that Cross does. This point is driven home by Cross's reaction to Lavender's death. Cross is not only a romantic who fantasizes a love affair that's not really there with Martha, he greatly exaggerates his responsibility for Lavender's death. The very randomness of Lavender's death—he is "zapped while zipping," shot after separating from the men briefly to urinate—belies Jimmy Cross's responsibility for the death. Cross blames himself for the death because, as the narrator tells us in a later story, "In the Field," "When a man died, there had to be blame." The soldiers wish to find a reason for the deaths they witness in order to make them less frightening, less random and meaningless. Blame can provide the illusion that war deaths such as those of Lavender and Kiowa are preventable, if only someone behaves differently, more responsibly, in the future. So, Cross determines that his love for Martha, his fantasies about her, are the cause of Lavender's death and that, to prevent such deaths in the future, he will strictly follow standard operating procedures and "dispense with love," focusing instead on duty. Ironically, Lavender dies after the platoon has just finished searching Viet Cong [Communist guerrillas in South Vietnam] tunnels, a tactic that *was* standard operating procedure, but an extremely dangerous undertaking. While Lee Strunk emerges intact from such a risky assignment, Ted Lavender dies a few moments later completely unexpectedly, while conducting the ordinary business of living.

Again, readers are supposed to see the irrationality of both Cross's burden of guilt as well as his resolve to be a better officer. In fact, it is his very refusal to question orders, to deviate from standard operating procedure, that leads him to camp in the "shitfield" later in the book and inadvertently brings about the death of Kiowa, another accident, and one which many different characters claim blame for. Readers, then, are not supposed to see Cross's burning of Martha's picture and renunciation of the imagination as "sad but necessary" consequences of war, but rather as the attempts of a romantic and guilt-ridden young man to gain control over a situation in which he actually has very little power. Because the burning of Martha's picture is linked to the burning of the Vietnamese village, readers see even more fully how mistaken and irrational Cross is in his reaction to Lavender's death.

"Love"

The second story in the collection, "Love," further complicates our view of "The Things They Carried." In "Love," readers are first introduced to the character of narrator Tim O'Brien who

After the death of one of the characters in Tim O'Brien's novel The Things They Carried, *Lieutenant Jimmy Cross refashions himself in the style of western film hero John Wayne (pictured).* Library of Congress.

remembers Jimmy Cross coming to talk to him at his home years after the war ended. Placed as it is immediately after the opening story and involving two of the same central characters (Martha and Jimmy Cross), "Love" comments on and draws attention to the fictive status of the previous story. In fact, readers discover, at the end of "Love," that the story "The Things They Carried" is written by narrator O'Brien, who explains,

> For the rest of his visit I steered the conversation away from Martha. At the end, though, as we were walking out to his car, I told him that I'd like to write a story about some of this. Jimmy thought it over and then gave me a little smile. "Why not?" he said. "Maybe she'll read it and come begging. There's always hope, right?"

> "Right," I said.

> He got into his car and rolled down the window. "Make me out to be a good guy, okay? Brave and handsome, all that stuff. Best platoon leader ever." He hesitated for a second. "And do me a favor. Don't mention anything about—"

> "No," I said, "I won't."

What about this silence that remains at the end of "Love"? When Cross begs O'Brien, "Don't mention anything about—," what does he mean? Is he referring to the death of Ted Lavender or is he hinting at some other event, one which O'Brien does remain silent about? While [critic] Lorrie Smith reads the ambiguity of this ending as indicative of a bond between the two men, who "wordlessly understand each other," it seems to me that the relationship between O'Brien and Cross is more complex. If Cross is referring here to Ted Lavender's death, must we not read O'Brien the narrator as betraying his friend? Even if O'Brien abides by his promise to Cross, repressing something even more troubling than Lavender's death, why the dark hint about some worse secret? Surely this betrays the spirit, if not the letter, of Cross's request. Even more, why include this vignette at all, except to complicate the previous story?

Author O'Brien deliberately juxtaposes these two stories to make readers question the perceptions presented in the previous story. Readers see that the events surrounding Lavender's death are filtered not only through Cross's subjective and guilt-laden impressions, but are then shaped into fiction by the Tim O'Brien character who may or may not be a reliable narrator. The fact that narrator O'Brien tells us about Cross's desire to come off as handsome and brave, the "best platoon leader ever," should deconstruct for readers Cross's macho resolves at the end of "The Things They Carried." Among other things, Cross determines not to fantasize about Martha anymore, to think about her only as belonging elsewhere. A new "hardness" develops in his stomach along with a new firmness to carry out his duties. He resolves to "be a man" about his responsibility for Lavender's death, confessing his culpability to his troops. He determines to love his men more than he loves women, yet to remain strong and distant from them, "leaving no room for argument or discussion" when he issues orders. Cross's intent here is to become, in many respects, the traditional American John Wayne–type hero, an icon of American individualism and courage who moves from the western frontier to the "new frontier" of Vietnam. In fact, the story ends with explicit frontier imagery as Jimmy Cross pictures his men "saddling up" and moving "west" under his command in the last line of the story. Even if narrator O'Brien is trying to fulfill Cross's request to come off as a stereotypical war hero, author O'Brien exposes the falseness of such constructs by laying bare his own devices.

A More Complex Portrait of Martha

The story "Love" also should make readers question the portrait of Martha presented in the previous story. In "Love,"

Martha still seems distant and alone as she was in "The Things They Carried," but she is no longer the dreamy poet of Cross's earlier imaginings. She is a trained nurse and a Lutheran missionary who has seen a great deal of the world, having served in Ethiopia, Guatemala, and Mexico, locales as exotic-sounding as Vietnam probably was to the young, inexperienced Jimmy Cross before his war years. When Cross tells Martha of his strangely violent yet tender college fantasy of tying her to the bed and stroking her knee all night, Martha replies that she can't understand "the things men do." Taken by itself, this moment seems to cement Martha's outsider status; while the narrator and Jimmy Cross understand each other, Martha is cold and unreceptive and only increases Cross's suffering. But the phrase "the things men do" first appears in the previous story, in the mind of Jimmy Cross after he determines to banish Martha from his thoughts:

> Henceforth, when he thought about Martha, it would be only to think that she belonged elsewhere. He would shut down the daydreams. This was not Mount Sebastian, it was another world, where there were no pretty poems or mid-term exams, a place where men died because of carelessness and gross stupidity. Kiowa was right. Boomdown, and you were dead, never partly dead.
>
> Briefly, in the rain, Lieutenant Cross saw Martha's gray eyes gazing back at him.
>
> He understood.
>
> It was very sad, he thought. The things men carried inside. The things men did or felt they had to do.
>
> He almost nodded at her, but didn't.

Martha's disapproval here is clearly a product of Cross's own guilt-ridden imagination. He pictures her "gray eyes gazing back at him" and condemning him silently for shutting her out. Surely the later scene's conscious echoing of the language used earlier should remind us that all of Cross's interactions with Martha are tainted by a masculine anxiety over his failure to be "the best platoon leader ever." Cross projects his anxiety and guilt onto his imaginary, disapproving Martha who cannot understand "the things men do." Yet, author-O'Brien painstakingly shows us that the failure to understand another person works both ways. When Martha tells Cross about her life since college—her missionary service and the fact that she never married—O'Brien writes that "it occurred to [Cross] that there were things about her he would never know." While her missionary background in the third world hints at hardship and self-sacrifice perhaps comparable to Cross's war experiences, neither Martha nor Jimmy Cross pursue a more detailed understanding of the other's life. The revised background on Martha should suggest to readers that she, too, had "things to carry," things that Cross cannot know anymore than those who were not in Vietnam can comprehend the war experience.

"Sweetheart of the Song Tra Bong" Redefines Women's Role in War

Katherine Kinney

Katherine Kinney has taught at the University of California, Riverside, and has published widely on the cultural impact of war.

In this selection, Katherine Kinney views O'Brien's story, "The Sweetheart of the Song Tra Bong," as a sophisticated and gender-redefining tale of a woman's descent into the jungles of Vietnam. Women's roles in warfare are traditionally characterized by their sexuality, Kinney says. In the character of Mary Ann Bell, however, O'Brien portrays a woman who trades her traditional role as a girlfriend for one more closely associated with males, while still retaining her femininity. Though Mary Ann may discard her conventional gender-related domestic and sexual stereotypes, Kinney claims that no Vietnamese women may participate in her liberation: In entering into the Vietnamese landscape, she symbolically displaces the native women. Thus her journey mirrors that of the American women's movement at the time, which had not yet confronted racial, national, and cultural differences.

Tim O'Brien's story "Sweetheart of the Song Tra Bong" offers a brilliant gloss of the gendered cultural logic of war stories. Framed as a tale told by a highly unreliable narrator, Rat Kiley, "Sweetheart" tells the impossible story of a girl who succeeds in "humping the boonies." A young medic at a small station in a remote mountain location of Vietnam sends his girlfriend a ticket to come visit him. Seventeen years old, fresh

Katherine Kinney, *Friendly Fire: American Images of the Vietnam War*, pp. 150–56. © 2000 by Oxford University Press, Inc. By permission of Oxford University Press, Inc.

out of high school, Mary Ann Bell arrives on a chopper in white culottes and a "sexy pink sweater," full of innocent curiosity and good cheer. The story presses two conflicting points of impossibility: whether a girl could get to "the boonies" and what would happen if she did. Getting her there, the resourceful young medic, Mark Fossie, explains, was expensive and "the logistics were complicated, but it wasn't like getting to the moon." Mary Ann Bell becomes another of O'Brien's travelers, like Paul Berlin in *Going After Cacciato*, who embarks on an improbable but eminently mappable journey. It is the issue of what happens when she arrives in country that far more seriously strains not simply the imagination but the gendered narrative boundaries of war itself.

Mary Ann Bell's trip to Vietnam violates every operative assumption regarding how and when and where and why women enter war stories. At first she plays the traditional role, mooning over her boyfriend, flirting just enough with the seven other medics and playing volleyball in "cut-off blue jeans and a black swimsuit top, which the guys appreciated." In short, "she was good for morale." The guys like her but also come to respect her; she asks good questions, "paid attention," and when casualties come in "Mary Ann wasn't afraid to get her hands bloody." She comes to feel "at home" in Vietnam. Besides her good-natured flirting and showing off her long legs, however, Mary Ann does nothing to make the camp seem more "like home." She does not cook or clean or offer any little domestic touches. Instead, her attention is drawn out of the camp, away from her boyfriend and his comfortably limited engagement with combat, and toward "those scary green mountains to the west." From the ARVN [Army of the Republic of Vietnam, also known as South Vietnam] soldiers camped at the perimeter she learns some Vietnamese, "how to cook rice over a can of Sterno, and how to eat with her fingers." The men tease her about going "native." She badgers Fossie into taking her to the nearby village over his objection that the Viet Cong [Communist guerrillas in South Vietnam] control it. She seems to know no fear.

"A real tiger," said Eddie Diamond. "D-cup guts, trainer bra brains."

"She'll learn," somebody said.

Eddie Diamond gave a solemn nod. "That's the scary part. I promise you. This girl will most definitely learn."

Eddie's comic bra-size metaphor speaks to the heart of the story's improbability and its power. Mary Ann moves deeper into the war without moving out of her gender identity as a woman. When the wounded come in, "she learned how to clip an artery and pump up a plastic splint, and shoot in morphine," fascinated by the "adrenalin buzz that went with the job . . . [when] you have to do things fast and right." Mary Ann gains confidence and focus; she seemed like a "different person." She learns to shoot and "Cleveland Heights seemed very far away." This difference intrudes into her relationship with Mark. They still sleep together and plan for the future but "her body seemed foreign somehow—too stiff in places, too firm where the softness used to be." At an obvious level, this hardening of her body suggests masculinization, but Mary Ann remains very much a desirable woman to Mark and to all the men. The more telling change is a narrative one—her new uncertainty in the story she had shared with Mark since grammar school: "that they would be married some day, and live in a fine gingerbread house near Lake Erie, and have three healthy yellow-haired children, and grow old and no doubt die in each other's arms and be buried in the same walnut casket." After three weeks in country Mary Ann begins to qualify: "Not necessarily three kids, she'd say. Not necessarily a house on Lake Erie. 'Naturally we'll still get married,' she'd tell him, 'but it doesn't have to be right away. Maybe travel first. Maybe live together. Just test it out, you know?" This change, associated in the story with the war, also speaks to the social transformation in traditional mores associated with the sexual revolution and women's liberation movements of the 1960s. Mary Ann has begun to question the inevitable logic of domesticity.

In very subtle and provocative ways, "Sweetheart of the Song Tra Bong" is a story of the women's movement: of one woman's move beyond naturalized [established] gender roles which brings to light deeper assumptions about gender relations and the larger sense of reality. As narrator, Rat is furiously defensive of the story's veracity:

> [T]he one thing [Rat] could not tolerate was disbelief. . . .
> "She wasn't *dumb*," he'd snap. "Young, that's all I said. Like
> you and me. A *girl*, that's the only difference, and I'll tell
> you something: it didn't amount to jack. I mean, when we
> first got here—all of us—we were young and innocent, full
> of romantic bullshit, but we learned pretty damn quick. And
> so did Mary Ann." "You've got to get rid of that sexist atti-
> tude," Rat later chides his listeners, knowing that it is their
> assumptions about women and not their experience of the
> war which condition their sense of the possible or the real,
> their ability to believe the story. Like all the stories in *The
> Things They Carried*, "Sweetheart" is as much about the na-
> ture of stories as about the nature of war. At the crucial dra-
> matic moment, Rat plays on his listeners' assumptions. Mark
> wakes Rat late at night; Mary Ann is gone and he assumes
> that she must be sleeping with someone else. Rat does a
> "body count" but all the men are sleeping alone. Rat inter-
> rupts his narration to ask his listeners, "Where is she?" One
> connoisseur of stories immediately knows: she's with the
> Green Berets [members of the US Army's special forces]
> that Rat had mentioned at the beginning of his tale who op-
> erate out of a hootch [hut] at the edge of the camp but gen-
> erally ignore the medics: "all that's got to be there for a *rea-
> son*. That's how stories work, man."

Allegiance to narrative form temporarily overrides gender assumptions, and, in any case, Mark's narrative, "she's sleeping with somebody," stands ready to recuperate more familiar patterns of possibility. But this assumption, too, proves wrong. "She wasn't sleeping with any of them," Rat explains. "At least not exactly. I mean, she was sleeping with *all* of them, more or less, except it wasn't sex or anything. They was just lying together, so to speak, Mary Ann and these six grungy weirded-out Green Berets." "Lying down how?" the skeptical and confused listeners ask. "Ambush. All night long. Mary Ann's out on f---in' *ambush*." That Rat stumbles over the sexual metaphor here is less a mark of his "bad habit" of interrupting the flow of his stories with "little clarifications or bits of analysis and personal opinions" than a measure of how deeply Mary Ann's actions have compromised narrative expectations and even possibility. Mary Ann has transgressed the boundaries of common sense in the deepest meaning of the term, the shared assumptions that create a sense of reality.

For common sense would surely suggest that whatever experience Mary Ann gains in Vietnam will necessarily be sexual. Going to Vietnam expands her horizons, her sense of herself and the world. Throughout the 1960s and beyond, sexual freedom has served as both the metaphor and the substance of all too many stories of women's liberation. The narrative that most directly maps the intersection of the Vietnam War and the contemporary shift in gender roles, the film *Coming Home*, plots Sally ([actress] Jane Fonda)'s personal growth as the move from the bed of her traditional soldier husband to that of the countercultural antiwar veteran. Sleeping with one of the "Greenies" is the expected way for Mary Ann to move beyond Eddie and escape the home he represents by acting out her fascination with the landscape of Vietnam. Moreover, "f---ing ambush" encodes the violent sexual threat of war for women: rape. Common sense would dictate that Mary Ann would need to take one lover as protector from the sexual voraciousness [greed] depicted in most representations of the war. In an all-male society women are expected to serve as objects of sexual barter.

But O'Brien plots Mary Ann's move to the Greenies with even more care than her plausible if improbable journey to Vietnam. Crucial here is the emphasis on learning, on acquiring competence and with it respect. Rat's insistence that they were all innocent once but "learned pretty damn quick" in country speaks to the authorial heart of war stories which traces the soldier's journey from innocence to experience, from home to war. By constructing a plausible fiction which takes Mary Ann to Vietnam, O'Brien undoes the narrative presumption that identifies home as the realm of the female and war as the domain of the male. Once in country, she is taken through the deeply familiar routines of learning about the land and the war, its rhythms and demands. The men listening to Rat's story cannot disavow her story without disavowing the terms that authorize their own telling of war stories—how they acquired their own knowledge.

Mary Ann's interest in the land becomes desire and her knowledge translates into narrative possibility, moving ultimately to the story's radical denouement [conclusion] in which Mary Ann humps the boonies. Tellingly, however, the term is never used directly. Rat underlines the weirdness of her arrival by saying, "She shows up with a suitcase and one of those plastic cosmetic bags. Comes right out to the boonies." By implication, the boonies are exactly that place where American women are not. But one of the things that makes her appearance at this remote base possible is that being stationed there involves "no humping at all." In practical terms it is light duty with no officers, but the break in the metaphorical association of "boonies" and "humping" at the beginning of the story is literally and figuratively what makes its narration of the impossible possible. This unhooking of the sexual metaphor is generally characteristic of O'Brien's style which, almost uniquely among veterans writing fiction about the war, does not rely on the hypersexual vernacular [dialect] of the grunt. If, according to [author] Michael Herr [in his Vietnam War memoir *Dispatches*], the feeling of being in a firefight is most closely akin to "the feeling you'd had when you were much, much younger and undressing a girl for the first time," then for Mary Ann to be out on "f---ing ambush" is, to say the least, highly ironic. But the incongruity in "Sweetheart" rebounds on the male listeners (Herr's "you" literatized in Rat's audience) rather than violently back onto her body. Compare the violent fate of women caught playing soldier in the war zone in [former marine Gustav Hasford's Vietnam War novel] *The Short-Timers* or . . . in [Vietnam veteran and author] Larry Heinemann's [novel] *Paco's Story*, novels that contain some of the war literature's most brilliant linguistic plays on and with obscenity.

Within the story both Mary Ann and Rat scrupulously avoid using overt sexual metaphors to explain the desire she feels for the war. Mary Ann uses the term "appetite." "Sometimes I want to *eat* this place, Vietnam," she explains. "I want to swallow this whole country—the dirt, the death—I just want to eat it and have it there inside of me." Certainly there are sexual inferences in this desire to consume; there very well may have to be sexual entendres [interpretations] for her experience to register as a war story. But she cannot respond to the land with the kind of explicit language used by Michael Herr, "kiss it, eat it, f--- it, plow it with your whole body" or even "pucker and submit," without reopening the barely suspended disbelief regarding what women can do in war. Women are typically assumed to be literally, rather than, like Herr, symbolically ravished by war. Rat's metaphor is similar: "Vietnam had the effect of a powerful drug," that is illicit, pleasurable, and dangerous, again like sex, but not quite sex.

Rat's ultimate metaphor for Mary Ann's experience echoes across the 1960s' language of sex, drugs, self-discovery, and the war alike; Vietnam becomes her "trip."

The endorphins start to flow, and the adrenaline, and you hold your breath and creep quietly through the moonlit nightscapes; you become intimate with danger: you're in touch with the far side of yourself, as though it's another hemisphere, and you want to string it out and go where ever the trip takes you and be host to all the possibilities inside yourself. . . . She wanted more, she wanted to penetrate into the mystery of herself. . . .

In a perverse way Mary Ann's trip answers directly [British author] Virginia Woolf's call [for female independence]—she moves away from domestic space, away from the future husband who presents himself as her identity and discovers herself in relation to the landscape and within herself. While Woolf would hardly endorse Mary Ann's claim to the masculine art of war and its colonial context, the story presses the textual and material implications of women's liberation. Mary Ann moves quite literally beyond Rat or, by implication, any man's narration. Rat infuriates his listeners by claiming he doesn't know what happened to her, but he finally presents an ending to his story based on rumor and conjecture. Like [the character] Sean Flynn in *Dispatches*, "Mary Ann Bell joined the missing."

The story's end makes her absence radically active and thus powerfully denies any nostalgic recuperation of her character.

But the story did not end there. If you believed the Greenies, Rat said, Mary Ann was still somewhere out there in the dark. Odd movements, odd shapes. Late at night, when the Greenies were out on ambush, the whole rain forest would seem to stare in at them—a watched feeling—and a couple of times they almost saw her sliding through the shadows. Not quite but almost. She had crossed over to the other side. She was a part of the land. She was wearing her culottes, her pink sweater, and a necklace of human tongues. She was dangerous. She was ready for the kill.

Mary Ann's defection marks her as the enemy, but the story refuses to enact the familiar terms which connect women's liberation and the soldier's betrayal. "Sweetheart" is insistently about Mary Ann's self-discovery and its effect on the masculine activity of telling war stories rather than on the lives of the men she leaves behind. The story works directly against the deeply misogynist [women-hating] assumptions that make Jane Fonda such a familiar icon of veterans' feelings of betrayal. Rather than hatred, Rat confesses his love for Mary Ann, because she has ceased to be like "those girls back home . . . clean and innocent" who will never understand what he has been through. "After the war, man, I promise you, you won't find nobody like her." Rat brings to the surface the contradictory structures of war narrative that ask women to heal and absolve men of experiences they are not allowed to know. The Greenies' haunting feeling of being watched asserts Mary Ann's subversive claim to knowledge and experience, just as her necklace of tongues testifies to her violently earned right to tell war stories. Mary Ann has passed Herr's "moment of initiation where you get down and bite the tongue off the corpse" and now sings in a language "beyond translation."

But if gender is denaturalized [made unnatural] as a system of absolute difference, Mary Ann's trip to the "far side of herself," especially as likened to "another hemisphere," also suggests more traditional patterns of imperial and racial otherness. The scene in which Mark and Rat confront Mary Ann in the Greenies' hootch is an orgy of hyperbolic [exaggerated] imagery that parodies [the character] Kurtz's compound in [the Vietnam War movie] *Apocalypse Now*: "tribal music," the "exotic" scent of incense mingling with the "stench of the kill," a decayed leopard's head, "strips of yellow brown skin" hanging from the rafters, and a poster that declares "in neat black lettering: ASSEMBLE YOUR OWN GOOK!! FREE SAMPLE KIT!!" Mary Ann emerges out of the gloom, wearing "her pink sweater and a white blouse and a simple cotton skirt." She is the same but clearly not the same. Her eyes are "utterly flat and indifferent," the mark of the proverbial thousand-yard stare.

> But the grotesque part, [Rat] said, was her jewelry. At the girl's throat was a necklace of human tongues. Elongated and narrow, like pieces of blackened leather, the tongues were threaded along a copper wire, one overlapping the next, the tips curled upward as if caught in some horrified final syllable.

If this scene is the clearest display of Rat's "reputation for exaggeration and overstatement," it also presents a deeply familiar pattern of horror, of, in fact, *the* horror, Kurtz's vision of the heart of darkness.

Mary Ann's desire to "penetrate deeper into the mystery of herself" rebounds ironically on a Modernist [from a literary movement that valued individualism over social forces] legacy that projects the bourgeois unconscious onto the colonized landscapes of Asia and Africa. In a deeply canny [clever] revision of [Polish-born British author Joseph] Conrad's [novel] *Heart of Darkness*, Mary Ann is both Kurtz and the Intended [Kurtz's admiring fiancée], liberating the woman from the drawing room where she is made to embody the hypocrisy of the imperial project. Mary Ann's "crossing over to the other side," which Rat describes not as joining the enemy's army but as "becoming part of the land," deconstructs [exposes contradictions in] the gendering of the boonies as both feminized landscape to be humped and the furthest distance from the home where the woman waits. But Mary Ann's identification with the land displaces the Vietnamese even as it makes manifest the gendered construction of the imperial landscape. The Vietnamese are literally dismembered, figured only as pieces of skin and the tongues Mary Ann has appropriated to voice her own experience. In particular, Mary Ann's claim to the landscape of the war displaces Vietnamese women, whose bodies stereotypically in American representations negotiate the relationship between war and sexuality, material and narrative violence in country. The exclusion of Vietnamese women from the story is a necessary condition of its narratability; their absence underwrites the construction of the boonies as the place where women are not and enables the gap between "humping" and "boonies." The "problem" that racial, national, and cultural difference poses in Mary Ann's liberation from the gendered conventions of war narrative is, not coincidentally, the problem the women's movement itself floundered on in the 1970s.

Homer's *Iliad* Provides Insights into O'Brien's *The Things They Carried*

Christopher Michael McDonough

Christopher Michael McDonough has taught at Sewanee: The University of the South, Boston College, and Princeton University. He is the author of Servius' Commentary on Book Four of Virgil's "Aeneid".

Christopher Michael McDonough asserts that the dilemma Tim O'Brien faces in The Things They Carried—*whether to fight or to flee the Vietnam War—is nothing new: Homer covered similar ground thousands of years ago in his epic poem* The Iliad. *In particular, Tim O'Brien finds himself in a situation similar to that of Homer's character Hector when Hector encounters certain defeat at the hands of Achilles. If Hector stays and fights, he will die. If he seeks safety, he will suffer certain shame. Ultimately, he runs around the walls of Troy, pursued by his Greek foe. O'Brien's heroes, such as the fictional Tim O'Brien and Norman Bowker, make gestures similar to Hector's. According to McDonough, both O'Brien and Homer powerfully dramatize the dichotomy of courage and cowardice that those who fight wars must confront.*

"The war, like Hector's own war, was silly and stupid."

—*Tim O'Brien,* If I Die in a Combat Zone

What has Troy to do with Vietnam? In recent years, the pertinence of the one Asian war to the other has been powerfully argued by numerous scholars, notably Jonathan Shay, in his seminal study, *Achilles in Vietnam: Combat Trauma*

Christopher Michael McDonough, "'Afraid to Admit We Are Not Achilles': Facing Hector's Dilemma in Tim O'Brien's *The Things They Carried*," *Classical and Modern Literature* 20-3, Spring 2000, pp. 23–32. Reprinted by permission.

and the Undoing of Character, as well as by various authors responding to Shay in a special issue of *Classical Bulletin* 71.2 (1995), "Understanding Achilles." As can be seen in the titles here mentioned, the critical emphasis has generally been laid on the experience of Achilles, while little attention has focused on what [classical scholar] James Redfield once called "the tragedy of Hector." Some discussion of the great Trojan hero might prove useful, however, especially for understanding Tim O'Brien's *The Things They Carried*, one of the finest works of American literature to emerge from the experience in Vietnam: for Hector as well as the protagonist of *The Things They Carried*, both brought to the brink by the necessity of battle, the dilemmas posed by the warrior mentality force unsettling questions about their societies and themselves.

To Fight or Flee

As it was for the many young men who opposed the war in Vietnam, the debate over whether to fight or to flee had been at once a personal and political one for O'Brien. After negatively assessing the justice of the American involvement in Indochina [mainland Southeast Asia], the narrator wonders whether it would be courageous or cowardly to fight for a cause he believed to be wrong. Although O'Brien elected to go to the war, the quandary remains in the foreground of his work: a central concern of *The Things They Carried*, a quasi-autobiographical work of fiction, is the shifting and indefinite line which divides bravery from cowardice (as well as honor from shame). "For the common soldier," O'Brien remarks in an oft-quoted sentence, ". . . the only certainty is overwhelming ambiguity." Many literary critics have rightly characterized O'Brien's uncertainty as postmodern, but in fact *The Things They Carried* deals with issues of courage as old as war itself—or at least as old as the oldest literature about war. In *If I Die in a Combat Zone*, an earlier work which anticipated many of the themes of *The Things They Carried*, O'Brien often turned to [Greek philosopher] Plato for enlightenment in these matters, citing definitions of courage from both the *Laches* and the *Republic* and applying them to his own situation in Vietnam. But in *The Things They Carried,* and especially in the chapters "On the Rainy River" and "Speaking of Courage," O'Brien discusses topics which might more profitably be considered from a Homeric rather than Socratic viewpoint.

As one scholar has noted of *The Things They Carried,* "There is nothing new in what O'Brien demonstrates here about trying to tell war stories ... and, of course, Homer's *Iliad* is the primal statement on the contradictions inherent in war." Some consideration of Homer's poetry can help to sharpen analysis of combat experience as, in fact, Jonathan Shay has shown in his aforementioned study of post-traumatic stress disorder. While much of *Things They Carried* likewise deals with the subsequent effects of combat, O'Brien also assesses the soldier's frame of mind *before* going off to war: in the book's first chapter, he lists not just the assorted weapons and supplies each soldier must carry while marching, but also "the emotional baggage of men who might die," thus delineating the things they carried mentally as well as physically. The contours of this state of mind are most vividly portrayed in "On the Rainy River," in which the narrator—"Tim O'Brien," a character distinct from the author—describes what he did after receiving his draft notice, in June, 1968, a few short weeks after his college graduation. At first enraged and then filled with self-pity, he spends an anxious month debating whether he should go to the war or flee his Minnesota home for Canada. One day, he snaps—a matter to be discussed more fully below—and drives north until he reaches the Rainy River; there he stops at the Tip Top Lodge, an abandoned resort on the American side of the border, run by an octogenarian named Elroy Berdahl. It is not anything which the old man says or does that is important for O'Brien during the agonizing days that follow—quite the opposite. Throughout this difficult time, the narrator is especially grateful for the "willful, almost ferocious silence" Berdahl maintains, a reprieve from the pressing voices which are described at various points in the episode. Before his flight north, for instance, he had thought of what might be said by the people of his conservative hometown:

> ... it was easy to imagine [them] sitting around a table at the old Gobbler Café on Main Street, coffee cups poised, the conversation slowly zeroing in on the young O'Brien kid, how the damned sissy had taken off for Canada.

It is ultimately in these voices that O'Brien locates the source of his anxiety: in addition to a fundamental disagreement about the war in Vietnam, his dilemma is a struggle between a well-founded fear of death and a profound feeling of being ashamed. As he writes,

> Intellect had come up against emotion. My conscience told me to run, but some irrational and powerful force was resisting, like a weight pushing me toward the war. What it came down to, stupidly, was a sense of shame. Hot, stupid shame. I did not want people to think badly of me. Not my parents, not my brother and sister, not even the folks down at the Gobbler Café.

To be at odds with public opinion was not an unusual position in 1968, to be sure. But while it would be wrong to reduce O'Brien's objections to the war to the mere desire to save his own skin, his remarks nonetheless take on meaningful perspective when compared with several episodes in the *Iliad* centering on the intertwined notions of glory and shame.

Glory and Shame in Homer's World

In his ground-breaking study, *The Greeks and the Irrational*, E.R. Dodds has noted, "Homeric man's highest good is not the enjoyment of a quiet conscience, but the enjoyment of

The characters in O'Brien's novel The Things They Carried *and those in Homer's epic poem* The Iliad *face similar situations.* Copyright © Oxford University Press 1960.

time, public esteem." This is not to say that the warriors at Troy are mindless automata surrendering all individuality to the whims of the crowd: in fact, they are acutely aware that the needs of the self and the demands of society may well be in conflict. James Redfield aptly puts it, "All men are born to die, but the warrior alone must confront this fact in his social life ... The greatness of Homer's heroes is a greatness not of act but of consciousness." There is a direct relationship in Homer's world between the risks one is willing to run and the respect society will confer; for this reason, the battlefield, where the threat to life is greatest, is the hero's proving ground. It is important to realize that the hero's status depends upon (and, in fact, cannot exist without) the tension between personal and public impulses: this tension is at the center of the epic. "The wrath of Achilles"—the words with which the *Iliad* famously open—is directed not at the Trojans but at Agamemnon, the commander who has arbitrarily stripped him of his war-bride, Briseis. As a woman, Briseis means little to the hero, but as a prize he has legitimately earned for valor in battle, her significance is immense. In this foolish exercise of power, Agamemnon unintentionally sets into motion a crisis about the nature of heroism which brings Achilles face-to-face with the hollowness of his shame culture: why should there be any personal risk, if there is to be no public recognition?

In addition to the possibility of winning glory, the Homeric hero is motivated also by *aidos*, "shame." By and large, this aspect of the ancient mentality is typified in the person of Hector, Achilles' great Trojan opponent. More than any other combatant at Troy, Hector is aware of his special status as a warrior: as the greatest hero on the Trojan side, he carries the greatest burden in its defense and has the greatest reputation to lose in any defeat. Nonetheless, Hector is only mortal and cannot overcome Achilles, the son of a goddess; Achilles' withdrawal, however, allows Hector to score enormous victories over the Greeks, culminating in the slaying of Patroclus. When

Achilles subsequently rejoins the battle, Hector has grown proud in his achievements and so ignores the advice of his brother Polydamas that he remove the troops from the field. What follows is a complete disaster for the Trojans: those who escape slaughter run headlong back to Troy, leaving Hector alone in Book Twenty-two to face the all-but-invincible Achilles. There, before the gates of Troy as the whole city watches from the walls, harsh reality begins to set in on Hector, who says to himself,

> Ah me, if I go now inside the gates and wall, Polydamas will be the first to reproach me, since he tried to convince me to lead the Trojans back to the city on that fateful night when godlike Achilles rose up. But I would not listen, though it would have been far better had I. Now since I have by my own stupidity destroyed my people, I am ashamed before the Trojans and the Trojan women in their trailing robes, that some lesser man than I will say of me, *Hector put his faith in his own strength, and destroyed his people.* That is what they will say. But for me, it would be much better then to confront Achilles, strike him down, and return, or else to be killed by him in glory before the city.

Generations of readers have rightly admired the determination of Hector to see this heroic challenge through to its fatal end; O'Brien himself writes in *If I Die in a Combat Zone* how hard it is to picture oneself "as the eternal Hector, dying gallantly." Hector's refusal to retreat, however, must not be judged according to a reductive [reduced] concept of bravery, but rather in terms of competing disincentives [deterrents], as identified succinctly by Redfield: "Hector's fear of death is overcome by his greater fear of disgrace."

Going in Circles

Although a very different set of political circumstances stands in the background, a similar fear of disgrace overtakes O'Brien as he agonizes on the Rainy River. Like Hector who envisions the ridicule of the Trojans, he imagines his entire community watching and yelling at him, an overwhelming sensation he cannot endure. "I would go to the war," he writes, "—I would kill and maybe die—because I was embarrassed not to." Perhaps somewhat harshly, O'Brien calls himself a coward for giving in to these voices; he knows, though, that he has only chosen the lesser of his fears, stating earlier in the book of soldiers in general, "It was not courage, exactly; the object was not valor. Rather, they were too frightened to be cowards." These thoughts are handled more fully in "Under the Mountain," a chapter from *If I Die in a Combat Zone*, in which the narrator's friend Erik discusses [American poet] Ezra Pound's "Hugh Selwyn Mauberley" while the pair are still in boot camp at Fort Lewis, Washington. "All this not because of conviction, not for ideology," Erik says,

> rather it's from fear of society's censure, just as Pound claims. Fear of weakness. Fear that to avoid war is to avoid manhood. We come to Fort Lewis afraid to admit we are not Achilles, that we are not brave, not heroes.

As a consideration of the theoretical roots of heroism shows, the warrior's status is etched round by fears: it is only a matter of which one to give in to, or *not* to give in to, as the case may be. In Book Twenty-two, Hector is quite literally backed up against a wall. Before him lies Achilles and certain doom, behind him the Trojans and intolerable derision. Although he toys temporarily with the fantasy of a settlement, between these options there really is no other—he can be either a dead hero or a live coward. But at the crucial moment, as Achilles bears down, Hector runs. It would be a misinterpretation to see this as the cowardly choice, for it is neither cowardly nor a choice: we must note that, caught between difficult options, Hector does not run back *inside* the walls of Troy but instead *around* them, in this way straddling the line between death and dishonor. Eventually, the goddess Athena fools him into thinking his brother has joined him for the fight; he stops, realizes the trick, and is killed. Nonetheless, Homer's portrait of Hector powerfully captures the unyielding nature of the heroic paradox: the poet renders the warrior's inability to decide in terms of a mad dash around a wall.

Something like this Homeric trope [metaphor] of indecision—Hector's going around in circles—is to be found in O'Brien's work, where it symbolizes much the same thing. In *If I Die in a Combat Zone*, for instance, he writes that, after getting his draft notice in 1968, "Late at night, the town deserted, two or three of us would drive a car around and around the town's lake, talking about the war. . . ." O'Brien has employed this image several times in his work, most notably in "Speaking of Courage" from *The Things They Carried*. In this vignette, the narrator's friend, Norman Bowker, having returned home from the war, spends the Fourth of July driving his father's car around a lake eleven times pondering an important failure of nerve he had experienced in Vietnam. In both places, O'Brien patterns the decision between cowardice or courage in terms much like Hector's run, as a repeated circular motion.

Wrestling with One's Conscience

Closer still in spirit to Hector's dilemma is O'Brien's own flight to the Canadian border in "On the Rainy River." Throughout the difficult time after getting his draft notice, the narrator feels in himself "a moral split," an overwhelming sensation which, though eventually growing to encompass the world around him, originates in a simple dichotomy: "Run, I'd think. Then I'd think, Impossible. Then a second later I'd think, *Run*." As he continues, "I feared the war, yes, but I also feared exile." Later in the summer, this sense of internal division manifests itself externally, when one day, as he remarks, "I felt something break open in my chest . . . a physical rupture—a cracking-leaking-popping feeling." As a result of this crisis—quite literally a breaking point—O'Brien suddenly takes off, driving north until he reaches Elroy Berdahl's Tip Top Lodge. When O'Brien first sees the old man, his sense of self-division is all the more reinforced, since Berdahl carries a small paring knife, and furthermore, as he notes,

> His eyes had the bluish gray color of a razor blade, the same polished shine, and as he peered up at me I felt a strange sharpness, almost painful, a cutting sensation, as if his gaze were somehow slicing me open.

While the narrator acknowledges that this sensation is a result in part of guilt, we might also see his description of Berdahl's gaze as the widening of his problem from the personal to the cosmic. So great is the crisis which O'Brien feels—so strong is his sense of the dilemma facing him—that he feels it is visible to the people he meets. Indeed, this "moral split" which has already affected his body he now even senses in the landscape, as he waits for resolution by "the Rainy River, which separates Minnesota from Canada, and which for me separated one life from another."

It is in this ambivalent region, poised between conflicting visions of his future—balanced precariously at the Tip Top, as it were—that O'Brien wrestles with his conscience. Here, where he describes himself as "half awake, half dreaming," his riven [split] mental state is figured strongly by his liminal [in-between] status: we might recognize that the dilemma which Hector in the *Iliad* faced (and never resolved for himself) was rendered in topographical terms, as it is here by O'Brien, who envisions himself "on the margins of exile," and "[g]etting chased by the Border Patrol." At this excruciating point in the narrative, Elroy Berdahl takes O'Brien out for a fishing trip on the highly symbolic Rainy River. As the small motorboat makes its way upstream, O'Brien realizes "that at some point we must've passed into Canadian waters, across that dotted line between two different worlds." The narrator surmises that, in bringing the situation to this point, Berdahl had taken him "to the edge" and would watch "as I chose a life for myself." He chooses Vietnam rather than Canada—that is, fight rather than flight—making the same decision Hector did, though by surviving, he avoids Hector's fate. In forcing O'Brien's decision between the difficult options before him, Berdahl reenacts the role which Athena had played in Hector's final moments, though the old man with the sharp gray eyes is more benevolent to his charge than the gray-eyed goddess had been. "He was a witness, like God, or like the gods," writes O'Brien, "who look on in absolute silence as we live our lives, as we make our choices or fail to make them."

Patterns Found in Homer

Though these gods seem more Lucretian [typical of Roman philosopher-poet Lucretius] than Homeric, perhaps the author has consciously drawn on the *Iliad* for these remarks. In this context, it is worth noting Homer's description of the divine audience watching Hector's final moments:

> It was a great man who fled, but far better he who pursued him rapidly, since here was no festal beast, no ox-hide they strove for, which are the prizes that are given men for racing. No, they are running for the life of Hector, breaker of horses. As when about the turnposts racehorses with uncloven hooves run at full speed, since a great prize is laid up for their winning, a tripod or a woman, in games for a man's funeral, so these two swept whirling about the city of Priam in the speed of their feet, while all the gods were looking upon them.

At his moment of crisis, O'Brien feels that he too is surrounded by a roaring stadium crowd "[l]ike some weird sporting event," and that the gaze of a civic pantheon which includes Abraham Lincoln, Saint George [England's patron saint], the U.S. Senate, and LBJ [American president Lyndon Baines Johnson], falls upon him. Numbered among these cultural luminaries is "a blind poet scribbling notes." Very likely this description refers to [American poet] Robert Frost's famous reading at the inauguration of President [John F.] Kennedy, but does not the epithet "blind" also bring to mind the blind poet of Chios [a Greek island], Homer himself?

As an issue of interpretation, however, it can hardly matter whether or not O'Brien alludes deliberately to Homer. Because all wars result in widespread destruction and death, survivors "shape their own discoveries of war into patterns first to be found in Homer," as classicist James Tatum once noted in *The Yale Review*. Both Homer and O'Brien portray the experience of those who must come to grips with the dilemma courage imposes: on the one hand is the loss of face, on the other, the loss of life. For Homer, the debate which rages within Hector's heart about these difficulties is dramatized as a race around the walls of a city which his hero cannot honorably enter. This same debate is felt inside Tim O'Brien's heart as well and manifests itself bodily, growing so large at last that it requires the natural and political boundary dividing a continent to describe it. In each work, the authors imagine such divisions of self in broadly geographical terms, as their protagonists negotiate the no-man's land between the antitheses described by O'Brien so well: "War makes you a man; war makes you dead."

True War Stories Have No Easy Answers

Milton J. Bates

Milton J. Bates has served as a professor of English at Marquette University. His books include Wallace Stevens: A Mythology of Self *and* Reporting Vietnam: American Journalism 1959–1975.

In this viewpoint, Milton J. Bates addresses the ways in which Tim O'Brien undermines traditional storytelling methods. Bates writes that O'Brien favors what French literary theorist Roland Barthes called the hermeneutic, *or the mysteries a story presents, over the* proairetic, *the traditional sequence of events that leads to a conclusion. Bates stresses that O'Brien's story does not give the reader a neatly tied-up ending, an approach that parallels how the Vietnam War dragged on. The date of its termination is impossible to pin down, especially for those veterans who will always live out the aftereffects of the war. The true war story is that which strikes the reader viscerally, in the stomach, Bates argues, even as the reader's mind understands the contradictions involved in the storytelling.*

Of all the Vietnam war stories told to date, Tim O'Brien's collection *The Things They Carried* is the most sophisticated inquiry into the reader-writer contract and the conventions of storytelling. Apart from the narrator, the book's preeminent storyteller is Rat Kiley. In "Sweetheart of the Song Tra Bong" Rat's performance is evaluated by the narrator and another member of the platoon, Mitchell Sanders. The narrator calls Rat's credibility into question even before he begins the story, remarking that Rat liked to "rev up the facts" for greater emotional impact. Yet he concedes that Rat never

Milton J. Bates, *The Wars We Took to Vietnam: Cultural Conflict and Storytelling.* Berkeley and Los Angeles: University of California Press, 1996. pp. 247–54. Reproduced by permission.

backed down from the details of this particular story. On the contrary, Rat invokes the ultimate claim to authority: "I *saw* it, man. I was right there." His credibility is further enhanced by the narrator's description of his mood as he tells the story. Rather than consciously "performing," he appears sad, troubled, and edgy. Halfway into the story, he reviews the terms of the narrative contract by asking Mitchell Sanders whether he can guess what happened to Mary Anne Bell the night she failed to return to her boyfriend's bunk. Sanders, recalling what Rat had said previously about the Green Berets [a branch of the US Army's special forces], supposes that she is with them because "That's how stories work, man."

How to Recognize a True War Story

As the story proceeds, however, Sanders becomes impatient with Rat on two counts. First, Rat dwells on the hermeneutic code [a mystery in the text] of the story at the expense of the proairetic [a narrative that creates plot]. "All these digressions," Sanders complains, "they just screw up your story's *sound*. Stick to what happened." Rat sticks more or less to what happened, the proairetic code, until he gets to the scene where he and Mary Anne's boyfriend find her in the Green Berets' hooch [hut], wearing a necklace of human tongues. There he seems about to break off the story, having told everything he knows from personal experience. Sanders is furious:

"You can't do that."

"Do what?"

"Jesus Christ, it's against the *rules*," Sanders said. "Against human *nature*. This elaborate story, you can't say, Hey, by the way, I don't know the *ending*. I mean, you got certain obligations."

Though Rat goes on to fulfill his duties as a storyteller, he emphasizes that the ending of his story has a different warrant [proof] than its beginning. His conclusion comes from the Green Berets, mediated by another party. The powerful and probably "revved up" closing image of Mary Anne as a jungle predator therefore requires an act of faith on the part of the listener: "If you believed the Greenies. . . ."

"Sweetheart" is typical of *The Things They Carried* in its self-consciousness about narrative credibility and convention. The book alternates between expounding the terms of the reader-writer contract and testing them. When both parties honor the contract, "How to Tell [i.e., narrate] a True War Story" is implicitly also "How to Tell [i.e., recognize] a True War Story."

In the piece just alluded to, Rat Kiley tries his hand at literary (as distinct from oral) narrative. When his best friend Curt Lemon is killed by a booby trap, he writes a long letter to Lemon's sister, recounting Lemon's zany exploits and telling what close friends they were. Read as a love story, Rat's intended form, the letter requires a response from Lemon's sister. She apparently reads the words but misconstrues the convention; she may even be offended by his language or the things that he says about her brother. In any case she fails to respond, and Rat disguises his hurt feelings with obscenity, calling her a "dumb cooze." Toward the end of the story, the narrator applies the same epithet to a woman who listens to his account of Rat shooting a baby water buffalo, because she too fails to recognize the love story behind the rage and gore. In desperation the narrator imagines himself retelling the story with all of the significant "facts" revised or presented as fiction. Perhaps then she will get the point.

By insisting repeatedly on the distinction between "story-truth" and "happening-truth," *The Things They Carried* undercuts the mimetic [imitative] authority of mere fact and event. Like [American author John Clark] Pratt's [novel] *Laotian*

Fragments, it also questions the warrant for documents of all kinds. Readers of [O'Brien' story] "In the Field" are privy to several versions of the letter that Lieutenant Jimmy Cross plans to write to Kiowa's father, explaining the circumstances of Kiowa's death. Were all of them to reach written form, they would be hard to reconcile with one another. Jimmy Cross himself is unable to specify the meaning or the emotional overtones of the documents (to use the term loosely) that he receives from his girlfriend: the letters signed "Love, Martha," two photos, and the pebble sent as an ambiguous "token of her truest feelings for him" ("The Things They Carried"). When Henry Dobbins's girlfriend sends him a Dear John letter [a letter from a girlfriend telling a guy she's breaking up with him], he must quickly revise the significance of her pantyhose, which he wears around his neck as a talisman, in such a way as to preserve their magical powers ("Stockings").

The Two Tim O'Briens

The most important documents in the book are the brief essays written by the narrator, "Tim O Brien." In some cases these are interwoven with anecdotes, as in "How to Tell a True War Story"; in other cases they occupy chapters by themselves, as in "Good Form." One is tempted to read these as nonfiction, since they resemble the sort of authorial rumination to be found in the *Paris Review* or the *New York Times Book Review*. Furthermore, the Tim O'Brien who writes them appears identical with the author of the book. He is, as he tells us several times, "forty-three years old, and a writer now." He grew up in Worthington, Minnesota, graduated from Macalester College, served as an infantry-man in the I Corps region [a zone of operations defined by the US military] of Vietnam, and wrote the books *If I Die in a Combat Zone* and *Going after Cacciato*. Yet in other respects the "Tim O'Brien" who narrates *Things*, including the "nonfictional" parts, is a fictional creation of the author. "Tim O'Brien" has a daughter named

Kathleen with whom he returned to Vietnam in the late 1980s. Tim O'Brien, we know from other sources, has no daughter; he returned to Vietnam for the first time in 1994 with a friend named Kate.

O'Brien apparently had several reasons for creating a narrator in his near-likeness. He claims that by giving his own name to the narrator, he was able to tap into feelings and memories that were otherwise inaccessible. He was also intrigued by the literary possibilities of reversing the procedure of "new journalists" [who included subjective accounts in their writings] like [American writer] Norman Mailer by importing fact—that is, documentation—into fiction. This strategy allows him to engage in a sometimes exasperating but ultimately productive struggle with the reader. The struggle begins even before the first story, with the disclaimer, acknowledgment, and dedication pages. It is presumably the author who writes the disclaimer ("This is a work of fiction. Except for a few details regarding the author's own life, all the incidents, names, and characters are imaginary") and the acknowledgments. But if the characters are all imaginary, why is the book dedicated to a half-dozen of them? Conventionally, dedications are nonfiction and the work of the author, even when they introduce works of fiction. Here, however, the dedication is the work of the fictional narrator, "Tim O'Brien." As such, it signals our entry into a realm where narrative conventions have to be renegotiated.

Questioning Plot and Narrative Authority

This renegotiation is, on one level, the plot of *The Things They Carried*. As [author Peter] Brooks points out [in his book *Reading for the Plot*], "plot" has an insidious meaning—denoting a secret, often evil scheme—that can be an aspect of the literary meaning as well. This is certainly the case in *Things*, where the narrator appears to be playing much the same kind of game with the reader that he plays with the woman in

"How to Tell a True War Story." He invites an uncritical response to a story, then mockingly withdraws the grounds of that response. "How to Tell," for instance, begins with the assertion "This is true" and ends with "None of it happened." In "The Man I Killed" the narrator tells in great detail how he felt after killing a young Viet Cong [a Communist guerrilla fighting in South Vietnam] with a grenade; he also alludes to the episode in several other stories and essay-like passages. Yet this does not prevent him from revising the story twice in "Good Form." First he says that most of the details in the first version are correct, but it was someone else who killed the young man. "But listen," he says then. "Even *that* story is made up." Actually, there were many dead bodies, men he had not killed and refused even to look at. Is it safe to believe this version, after being taken in by two others? One has cause to reserve judgment, especially since the chapter ends with an exchange between the narrator and his fictitious daughter.

In the context of *The Things They Carried* as a whole, "The Man I Killed" invites us to reassess not only the nature of narrative authority and the kind of truth to be found in stories but also our Aristotelian [after the Greek philosopher Aristotle] assurance that we can identify beginnings and endings. Where does "The Man I Killed" begin—on the first page of the story, or in a snatch of dialogue that appears a hundred pages earlier? Does it end on the last page of the story or in an allusion a hundred pages later, at the beginning of another story?

An Assault on Closure

O'Brien mounts his most sustained assault on our conventional notions of closure in the sequence of stories dealing with Kiowa's death in a field of human waste, a paddy that the villagers use as a toilet. The first, "Speaking of Courage," is a literary exhibit, a model of the well-wrought short story typically found in classroom anthologies. Students would be cajoled or impressed into admiring the symmetries of the piece: Norman Bowker, a veteran of Vietnam, unable to tell his war story to his father, who is equally reticent about *his* war; the flares and mortars of Vietnam versus the fireworks of a small-town Fourth of July celebration; an Iowa lake with algae bloom juxtaposed against the muddy Song Tra Bong River; a drive-in intercom that sounds like a military field radio. Like Bowker's Chevy in its revolutions around the lake, the narrative traces a circle that neatly contains all of its parts.

In the very next chapter, however, the symmetry comes undone. "Tim O'Brien" tells how one letter from Bowker prompted him to write the story and how another prompted him to rewrite it in a manner more in keeping with "the full and exact truth about our night in the shit field." Bowker serves as "O'Brien's" literary conscience, playing Mitchell Sanders to his Rat Kiley. The last four sentences of "Notes" nevertheless imply that even this version of the truth is neither full nor exact: "In the interests of truth . . . I want to make it clear that Norman Bowker was in no way responsible for what happened to Kiowa. Norman did not experience a failure of nerve that night. He did not freeze up or lose the Silver Star for valor. That part of the story is my own." The phrase "my own" is tantalizing but ambiguous. Does it mean "something I made up" or "about me"?

Both meanings apply, as it turns out: the narrator projected onto Bowker his own feelings of complicity in Kiowa's death. As the story is revised in "In the Field," Bowker finds Kiowa's body but is not the one who allows his friend to sink beneath the ooze and suffocate. The guilty party—to use a phrase that becomes problematic in a story where everyone and no one is finally guilty—is a character described simply as "the young soldier." It was he who had turned on his flashlight just before the mortar round struck, to show Kiowa a photograph of his girlfriend. Rationally speaking, this breach of light discipline had nothing to do with Kiowa's death, since a mortar cannot be aimed so quickly or accurately. But the young soldier still feels guilty according to a *post hoc propter hoc* [attributing a false cause to events] logic. Though he is never identified—even Lieutenant Jimmy Cross, who prides himself in treating his men as individuals, cannot remember his name—circumstantial evidence suggests that he is the narrator. The passage describing the young soldier's "tug-of-war" with Kiowa's boot duplicates the one featuring Bowker in "Speaking of Courage," and in the final chapter of *Things* the narrator says, "I watched my friend Kiowa sink into the muck along the Song Tra Bong."

The match between the narrator and the young soldier is imperfect, since "Tim O'Brien" is represented as older and more sophisticated than the kid with a girlfriend (former girlfriend, really) named Billie. Yet we infer that guilt motivates his return to the waste field with his daughter twenty years later, looking for "signs of forgiveness or personal grace or whatever else the land might offer." As told in "Field Trip," the narrator's story of his postwar adjustment differs considerably from that in "Notes." In the earlier chapter, he contrasts Bowker's anguish and aimlessness with his own graceful transition from Vietnam to Harvard and a successful career as a writer. But in "Field Trip" he speaks of an emotional numbness and loss of direction dating from Kiowa's death. His ritual of expiation, burying Kiowa's hatchet, does elicit the forgiveness he seeks. "In a way," he muses, "maybe, I'd gone under with Kiowa, and now after two decades I'd finally worked my way out."

The "Speaking of Courage" sequence, like the stories linked to "The Man I Killed," forces us to confront the arbitrariness of story endings. For Aristotle a satisfactory ending is one that "follows something else but nothing follows it." Though it is hard to imagine a war story in which nothing truly "follows" in the way of personal and social consequences, Aristotle praises [ancient Greek epic poet] Homer for selecting episodes from the Trojan War that could be manageably plotted. Vietnam storytellers are faced with the same problem of selecting what, in [American author] Henry James's phrase, "hangs together." Even as they contrive endings, they sometimes cannot resist drawing attention to the deus ex machina [a literary device wherein a problem is abruptly solved in a contrived manner]. . . .

At the Mercy of an Unreliable Narrator

O'Brien distrusts narrative closure because it violates our experience of life. In a novel published after *The Things They Carried*, entitled *In the Lake of the Woods* (1994), he offers several hypotheses regarding the disappearance of the two main characters but no definitive answers. He refuses to solve the mystery because, he asserts in a footnote, "truth won't allow it. Because there *is* no end, happy or otherwise. Nothing is fixed, nothing is solved." Perhaps for that reason O'Brien takes a step beyond [*The Quiet American* author Graham] Greene and [*In Country* author Bobbie Ann] Mason in *Things*, showing how the "happy" or "sweet" or otherwise gratifying conclusion can be reopened at will. This strategy is especially appropriate for stories about a war whose ending is no less in doubt than its beginning. Was it over in 1973, when the last American troops were withdrawn from Vietnam? In 1975, when South Vietnam fell to the North? In 1991, when President [George H.W.] Bush declared that the United States had "kicked the Vietnam syndrome once and for all" with its victory in the Persian Gulf? In 1995, when President [Bill] Clinton extended full diplomatic recognition to the government in Hanoi? Or will the war last as long as there are people whose lives have been affected by it?

In the process of challenging narrative closure, O'Brien also invites us to examine the kind of confidence we invest in storytellers. We are at the mercy of an unreliable narrator in *The Things They Carried*, if by "unreliable" we mean a storyteller who refuses to give us a single, consistent version of events. Yet the experience of listening to "Tim O'Brien" can be productive as well as exasperating if we reflect on how his unreliability affects us. . . .

The authority of *Things* derives . . . from the author's skill at creating powerful illusions and the reader's willingness to suspend disbelief, if only for the duration of the story. O'Brien supplies the reader with a field guide to the war story in "How to Tell a True War Story," which lists the structural and linguistic qualities of the genre and supplies illustrations. But he ultimately defines the true war story, much as Aristotle defined tragedy, according to its effect on the listener. Whether or not it recounts historically verifiable events, whether or not it is self-consistent, the true war story "makes the stomach believe." If the listener can summon the detachment to ask whether it is really true, it is not true in a way that O'Brien considers meaningful. But no sooner does the stomach believe than the brain is engaged and the once irresistible story becomes untenable. In *Things* as in every sphere of "real" life, illusions are continually being sustained and discredited, remade and rebroken.

O'Brien Offers No Resolution at the Conclusion of His Book

Robin Blyn

Robin Blyn has taught English at Westfield State College in Massachusetts and at the University of West Florida. She has published widely on the subject of American literature and culture.

In the following essay, Robin Blyn examines the ending of The Things They Carried *and finds that the book ultimately resists the type of closure that we expect from a story, especially the traditional war story. Blyn cites literary historian Paul Fussell's seminal book on war,* The Great War and Modern Memory, *in which Fussell suggests that the war story traditionally ends with a "reconsideration": both author and reader discover deeper insights into the human condition through the war experience. Blyn states that although O'Brien promises such reconsideration at the beginning of his final story "The Lives of the Dead," the book ends without resolution. The continuing images of "spin" and "loops" in the novel suggest the Vietnam veteran's unending immersion in the trauma of the war experience that even storytelling, despite its promise and power, cannot resolve.*

"But this too is true," Tim O'Brien's narrator insists in the first line of the chapter that concludes *The Things They Carried*: "Stories can save us." Entitled "The Lives of the Dead," this final chapter thus begins with a promise not only of healing, but of redemption as well. Stories, the narrator suggests, can heal the traumatized veteran of the Vietnam War and provoke an amnesiac nation into "working through" its troubled past. If, as John Hellmann [author of *American Myth and the Legacy of Vietnam*] has written, "the legacy of Vietnam is the disruption of our story, of our explanation of the past and vision of the future," then O'Brien's narrator apparently points "the disrupted story" and the nation toward a narrative cure. Such a reading of *The Things They Carried*, however, requires a denial of the novel's insistent destabilization of the "true" and its dogged attempts to render war unequivocally beyond redemption. Shifting attention from the final chapter's first line to its concluding passage makes visible the extent to which the novel challenges the narrative cure that its narrator ostensibly affirms.

An Unfulfilled Promise

The idea of stories as a curative force is attractive, particularly because it suggests that, as a collection of stories about American soldiers in Vietnam, *The Things They Carried* performs the narrative cure it prescribes, redeeming the reader and the writer at once. Prepared to be "saved," the producer and the receiver of the stories are poised for the closure traditionally accomplished in the final chapter of a war story. For, as [literary historian] Paul Fussell explains in his *The Great War and Modern Memory*, the third and final stage of the war narrative is the "reconsideration," in which the pro-war understanding of the world is replaced by the deeper insights made painfully clear by the war experience. Closure entails both a loss of innocence and redemption in the form of a richer appreciation for the complexities of the human condition. By beginning the final chapter with an assertion that "stories can save us," O'Brien apparently promises just this kind of "reconsideration." To the contrary, however, the chapter concludes with an image of suspension and spin while ice-skating that reflects a profound sense of cultural ambiguity. It is an image that recalls the critique of narrative structure first undertaken in chapter 3, aptly entitled "Spin," and expanded on four chapters later in "How to Tell a True War Story."

At the end of "The Lives of the Dead," an older "Tim" imagines a younger "Timmy" skating on a frozen lake with his childhood sweetheart, Linda. Tim writes:

> I'm young and happy. I'll never die. I'm skimming across the surface of my own history, moving fast, riding the melt beneath the blades, doing loops and spins, and when I take a high leap into the dark and come down thirty years later, I realize it is as Tim trying to save Timmy's life with a story.

Because this is the passage with which the novel concludes, the question of whether or not Tim is ultimately able to save his younger self "with a story" remains unresolved. Moreover, the reference to "loops" and "spins" links this image both to the circular path of memory and to the problem of the narrative "spin" known as "the war story." In the chapter entitled "Spin," the unending repetitions of the memory "loop" function as a check against the falsifications of the war story and its conventional "spins."

As a chapter, "Spin" exposes the desire that generates the genre of the war story, a dangerous and insipid desire to redeem what the narrator calls the "waste" of war. Like "The Lives of the Dead," it begins with a statement that the rest of the chapter throws into question. "The War wasn't all terror and violence," the narrator tells us. "Sometimes things could almost get sweet." What follows, however, is a series of vignettes that are anything but "sweet." When a Vietnamese boy with a plastic leg approaches an American soldier with a chocolate bar, the soldier reflects, "One leg, for Chrissake. Some poor [f---er] ran out of ammo." When the same soldier steals his friend's puppy, "strapped it to a Claymore antipersonnel mine and squeezed the firing device," he responds with an ironic affirmation of the initiation rite of the conventional war story: "What's everyone so upset about? . . . I mean, Christ, I'm just a *boy*." Here, the novel renders ironic both the loss of innocence and the "reconsideration" that structure the traditional war story. The positive spin that underlies the war story as a genre emerges here only as a bankrupt fantasy. Thus in "How to Tell a True War Story," the narrator warns, "If a story seems moral, do not believe it. If at the end of a war story you feel uplifted, or if you feel that some small bit of rectitude has been salvaged from the larger waste, then you have been made the victim of a very old and terrible lie." Aimed at exposing this "old and terrible lie," these chapters refute any narrative structure that would redeem the war, the storyteller, or the audience to which it is directed.

Resisting Closure

Against the comforts and closure of the war story, "Spin" reveals the circular repetitions and reenactments of traumatic memory. In "Spin," memory itself is depicted as a loop:

> The memory-traffic feeds into a rotary up on your head, where it goes in circles for a while, then pretty soon imagination flows in and the traffic merges and shoots down a thousand different streets. As a writer, all you can do is pick a street and go for the ride, putting things down as they come at you. That's the real obsession. All those stories.

Evoking the compulsive repetitions of traumatic memory, the narrator here characterizes stories not as the road to closure, but as "obsession," a kind of psychological "traffic." Effectively, this loop describes the structure of "Spin" and of *The Things They Carried* as a whole. For in place of tales of moral uplift and the persistence of human goodness, tales structured to provide the catharsis [a purifying emotional release] of Aristotelian tragedy, "Spin" offers the ambiguous, the unfinished, and the wound that will not succumb to the narrative cure. Keeping the wound open, O'Brien's text prevents the neat closure and false redemption of the traditional war story.

Given that the "spin" and the "loop" are terms central to the novel's critique of war stories and their specious attempts to reclaim meaning from the war experience, the final passage of "The Lives of the Dead" may be seen as a direct challenge to the sentence that begins it. Rather than confirming that "stories can save us" by redeeming the past and healing all wounds, Timmy's acrobatic performance on the frozen pond may be seen as a reiteration of the "memory-traffic" and its obsessive art. Prohibiting closure, *The Things They Carried* keeps the past from disappearing into the dead clichés of the war story, replacing redemption with a critical engagement with the past.

Social Issues in Literature

CHAPTER 3

Contemporary Perspectives on War

We Must Not Repeat the Mistakes We Made in Vietnam

Robert J. Bresler

Robert J. Bresler has served as national affairs editor of USA To-day *magazine and as a professor of public policy at Pennsylvania State University at Harrisburg. Among his books is* Us vs. Them: American Political and Cultural Conflict from WWII to Wa-tergate.

In this viewpoint, Robert J. Bresler asserts that political ideology shapes how we view any particular war, citing as examples Viet-nam and Iraq. Depending on ideology, Vietnam was either a war we had no business entering or a moral war fought against the Communist powers of China and the Soviet Union as well as the North Vietnamese. Pulling out of Vietnam, Bresler suggests, emboldened the Communist powers. Although America eventu-ally recovered from Vietnam, failing to win the war in Iraq may have more dire consequences. The war in Iraq measures our will, Bresler contends: Either we believe in American values or we do not, and our response to Iraq tests this elemental notion.

One's view of the past is shaped by the present, just as one's view of the present is shaped by the past. So it is with Vietnam and Iraq. The doves [peace supporters] that op-pose the war in Iraq have one history of the Vietnam War, just as the hawks [war advocates] that support the war in Iraq have another.

The Doves Version

Vietnam was a foolish intervention into a civil war we did not understand and never could win (or, for those on the far left, one we never should win). Wisdom only entered into the

Robert J. Bresler, "The Specter of Vietnam," *USA Today* (magazine), 135-27/42, March 2007, p. 9. Reprinted by permission of Society for the Advancement of Education.

tragedy when the U.S. decided to leave—mandated by a congressional cut-off of funds. The consequences of this mandate were, therefore, beneficial. Congress was emboldened to assert its power in foreign policy—passing the War Powers Resolution [which required the president to seek congressional authorization before sending troops abroad], limiting the power of the CIA to conduct covert operations and, thus, avoiding future Third World involvements. In the late 1970s, Congress also reduced the defense budget and cut off aid to the anti-Communist forces in Angola. The doves' lesson from Vietnam was that the U.S. was the cause of its own problems in the world and, if we reduced our military profile, most problems could be handled peaceably. We needed to understand our enemies and reduce their paranoia about us. With dovish opinion prevailing after Vietnam, detente [the relaxation of tensions] with the Soviet Union became a central priority of both the [Gerald] Ford and [Jimmy] Carter administrations.

The Hawks Version

Vietnam never was a civil war. The Vietcong [Communist guerrillas fighting in South Vietnam] were controlled by the North Vietnamese regime which, in turn, was financed and supported by the Soviets and Chinese. The U.S. did not lose the war on the battlefield. The Tet offensive [a major North Vietnamese military action against targets in South Vietnam], followed by the American counterattack, was a devastating defeat for the Vietcong. Yet, thanks to CBS anchor [and influential journalist] Walter Cronkite and the media commentators who parroted his line, the American public considered it a defeat. The war, according to this version, might have been won in 1968, by accepting Gen. William Westmoreland's [commander of US troops in Vietnam] recommendation for an additional 200,000 troops to finish the job or, in 1973, by continuing to support the South Vietnamese government after the North violated the 1973 truce agreement. The loss of Vietnam was a political one. A weakened Pres. Richard Nixon had to accede to Congress' wishes in the summer of 1973. By that time, not only had most of the Democrats given up on Vietnam, so had most of the Republicans. Pres. Gerald Ford, in the spring of 1975, when faced with the imminent collapse of the South Vietnamese resistance, could find little support for coming to their aid from either Republicans or Democrats. This defeat had anything but salutary [healthy] consequences. In its aftermath, the Soviets felt heartened enough to expand their influence in Angola, Ethiopia, and Nicaragua, boldly invade Afghanistan, modernize their intermediate range missile force, and continue their arms buildup. By the end of the 1970s, many thought the correlation of forces was tipping toward the Soviet Union. Only during the Ronald Reagan years did the U.S. eventually recover its footing.

Implications for Iraq

What are the historical lessons? Those who support an exit strategy for Iraq endorse the doves version of Vietnam. Some already are discussing how the U.S. should handle the problem of Iraqi refugees—especially those who stood with us during conflict—once we withdraw our forces. As [political columnist] David Ignatius wrote in *The Washington Post*, "Whatever we do in Iraq in [the] coming months, it should include a bipartisan commitment to keep faith with the people who risked everything for a new Iraq—by making room for them in America, if necessary. We need a surge of compassion more than a surge of U.S. troops." These doves appear unconcerned about the overall consequences of another American defeat.

There seems to be much wishful thinking about the matter; just as there were such "revelations" from the doves about the overall consequences of a withdrawal from Vietnam. Perhaps some war critics may see our leaving Iraq as just a tactical retreat in the war against terror from which we can recover, and would have the U.S. place its military focus upon Afghanistan (until, of course, the casualities become too high). Other dovish critics see the terrorist threat as one that requires only defensive measures by the U.S. and would demand any regime change efforts be sanctioned by the United Nations.

Those who support a victory strategy for Iraq fear the hawks version of Vietnam will repeat itself. With the majority of Democrats in Congress supporting a withdrawal and more Republicans coming to that view, hawks see the same collapse of political will that occurred in 1975. Pres. [George W.] Bush is determined to avoid such history, regardless of public opinion and the views of Congress. This is high stakes poker. As the Hoover Institution's [conservative columnist] Victor Davis Hanson wrote, "Imagine this war as a sort of grotesque race. The jihadists [used here to mean Muslim extremists] and sectarians [advocates of violent conflict along religious or political lines] win if they can kill enough Americans to demoralize us enough that we flee before Iraqis and Afghans stabilize their newfound freedom. They lose if they can't. Prosperity, security and liberty are the death knell to radical Islam. It's that elemental."

Should Pres. Bush's victory strategy fail to bring results by the end of this year [2007], he may be as powerless as Richard Nixon was in 1973. Could we recover from such a defeat, as we eventually did from Vietnam, after 10 difficult years? History never quite repeats itself in the same way, and this time we may not be so fortunate. This enemy has no fear of death, moral inhibitions, government to protect, or empire to preserve. Destruction of the West has become an end in itself. This war is above anything else a test of will. Either we believe in ourselves, our strength, and our values or we don't. As Hanson put it, "It's that elemental."

The Vietnam and Iraq Wars Are Indefensible

John Pilger

John Pilger is an Australian journalist and documentary film-maker based in London. His films about Vietnam include The Quiet Mutiny, Vietnam: Still America's War, Do You Remember Vietnam?, *and* Vietnam: The Last Battle.

According to John Pilger, the Vietnam and Iraq Wars are examples of Western aggression directed at Eastern cultures and both wars are morally corrupt and irresponsible. Yet thirty years of English and American propaganda, which has found its way into history books and school curricula, has perpetuated myths about the Vietnam conflict. Pilger maintains that this propaganda tends to portray the Vietnam War in black and white terms, with the good democratic forces of the West fighting the evil Communists of the East. Pilger sees the same simplifications and morally indefensible logic in the lead-up to the Iraq conflict, and he believes that in both wars thousands of innocent lives have been lost to Western aggression.

How does thought control work in societies that call themselves free? Why are famous journalists so eager, almost as a reflex, to minimise the culpability of a prime minister who shares responsibility for the unprovoked attack on a defenceless people [the Iraqis], for laying waste to their land and for killing at least 100,000 people, most of them civilians, having sought to justify this epic crime with demonstrable lies? What made the BBC's [British Broadcasting Company's] Mark Mardell describe the invasion of Iraq as "a vindication for him"? Why have broadcasters never associated the British or

John Pilger, "John Pilger Finds Our Children Learning Lies," *New Statesman*, February 21, 2005. Reprinted by permission.

American state with terrorism? Why have such privileged communicators, with unlimited access to the facts, lined up to describe an unobserved, unverified, illegitimate, cynically manipulated election [in 2005 in Iraq; the first multiparty election in fifty years], held under a brutal occupation, as "democratic", with the pristine aim of being "free and fair"? That quotation belongs to Helen Boaden, the director of BBC News.

Historical Amnesia

Have she and the others read no history? Or is the history they know, or choose to know, subject to such amnesia and omission that it produces a world-view as seen only through a one-way moral mirror? There is no suggestion of conspiracy. This one-way mirror ensures that most of humanity is regarded in terms of its usefulness to "us", its desirability or expendability, its worthiness or unworthiness: for example, the notion of "good" Kurds in Iraq and "bad" Kurds in Turkey. The unerring assumption is that "we" in the dominant West have moral standards superior to "theirs". One of "their" dictators (often a former client of ours, such as Saddam Hussein) kills thousands of people and he is declared a monster, a second Hitler. When one of our leaders does the same he is viewed, at worst, like [English prime minister Tony] Blair, in Shakespearean terms. Those who kill people with car bombs are "terrorists"; those who kill far more people with cluster bombs are the noble occupants of a "quagmire".

Historical amnesia can spread quickly. Only ten years after the Vietnam war, which I reported, an opinion poll in the United States found that a third of Americans could not remember which side their government had supported. This demonstrated the insidious power of the dominant propaganda, that the war was essentially a conflict of "good" Vietnamese against "bad" Vietnamese, in which the Americans became "involved", bringing democracy to the people of southern Vietnam faced with a "communist threat". Such a false and dishonest assumption permeated the media coverage, with honourable exceptions. The truth is that the longest war of the 20th century was a war waged against Vietnam, north and south, communist and non-communist, by America. It was an unprovoked invasion of the people's homeland and their lives, just like the invasion of Iraq. Amnesia ensures that, while the relatively few deaths of the invaders are constantly acknowledged, the deaths of up to five million Vietnamese are consigned to oblivion.

Distortions of the Truth

What are the roots of this? Certainly, "popular culture", especially Hollywood movies, can decide what and how little we remember. Selective education at a tender age performs the same task. I have been sent a widely used revision guide for GCSE [general certificate of secondary education] modern world history, on Vietnam and the cold war. This is learned by 14- to-16-year-olds in our schools. It informs their understanding of a pivotal period in history, which must influence how they make sense of today's news from Iraq and elsewhere.

It is shocking. It says that under the 1954 Geneva Accord: "Vietnam was partitioned into communist north and democratic south." In one sentence, truth is despatched. The final declaration of the Geneva conference divided Vietnam "temporarily" until free national elections were held on 26 July 1956. There was little doubt that [Vietnamese communist revolutionary] Ho Chi Minh would win and form Vietnam's first democratically elected government. Certainly, President [Dwight] Eisenhower was in no doubt of this. "I have never talked with a person knowledgeable in Indo-Chinese affairs," he wrote, "who did not agree that . . . 80 per cent of the population would have voted for the communist Ho Chi Minh as their leader."

Not only did the United States refuse to allow the UN to administer the agreed elections two years later, but the "demo-

Many similarities can be drawn between the Vietnam and Iraq Wars. Some view both wars as morally corrupt and irresponsible. © EditorialFotos/Alamy.

cratic" regime in the south was an invention. One of the inventors, the CIA official Ralph McGehee, describes in his masterly book *Deadly Deceits* how a brutal expatriate mandarin [bureaucrat], Ngo Dinh Diem, was imported from New Jersey to be "president" and a fake government was put in place. "The CIA," he wrote, "was ordered to sustain that illusion through propaganda [placed in the media]."

Phoney elections were arranged, hailed in the west as "free and fair", with American officials fabricating "an 83 per cent turnout despite Vietcong [Communist guerrillas in South Vietnam] terror". The GCSE guide alludes to none of this, nor that "the terrorists", whom the Americans called the Vietcong, were also southern Vietnamese defending their homeland against the American invasion and whose resistance was popular. For Vietnam, read Iraq.

Simplified Good and Evil

The tone of this tract is from the point of view of "us". There is no sense that a national liberation movement existed in Vietnam, merely "a communist threat", merely the propaganda that "the USA was *terrified* that many other countries might become communist and help the USSR—they didn't want to be *outnumbered*", merely that President Lyndon B Johnson "*was determined to keep South Vietnam. communist-free*" (emphasis as in the original). This proceeds quickly to the Tet Offensive [a North Vietnamese military operation targeting the populated areas of South Vietnam] of 1968, which "ended in the loss of thousands of American lives—14,000 in 1969— most were young men". There is no mention of the millions of Vietnamese lives also lost in the offensive. And America merely began "a bombing campaign": there is no mention of the greatest tonnage of bombs dropped in the history of warfare, of a military strategy that was deliberately designed to force millions of people to abandon their homes, and of chemicals used in a manner that profoundly changed the environment and the genetic order, leaving a once-bountiful land all but ruined.

This guide is from a private publisher, but its bias and omissions reflect that of the official syllabuses, such as the syllabus from Oxford and Cambridge, whose cold war section refers to Soviet "expansionism" and the "spread" of communism; there is not a word about the "spread" of rapacious America. One of its "key questions" is: "How effectively did the USA contain the spread of communism?" Good versus evil for untutored minds.

"Phew, loads for you to learn here . . ." say the authors of the revision guide, "so get it learned right now." Phew, the British empire did not happen; there is nothing about the atrocious colonial wars that were models for the successor power, America, in Indonesia, Vietnam, Chile, El Salvador, Nicaragua, to name but a few along modern history's imperial trail of blood of which Iraq is the latest.

And now Iran? The drumbeat has already begun. How many more innocent people have to die before those who filter the past and the present wake up to their moral responsibility to protect our memory and the lives of human beings?

The Vietnam War Is Still with Us

Peter Edidin

Peter Edidin has served as an editor for the New York Times. *He writes regularly about culture and the arts.*

According to Peter Edidin, even though the Vietnam War ended over thirty years ago, we are still living with its aftermath. The media coverage of the war effort had a profound bearing on events. Although the US government insisted that the war was going well, television reporting continued to depict the carnage to a squeamish nation. This coverage, Edidin writes, had the effect of dividing the American public's attitude toward Vietnam in a manner never before seen during wartime. The continuing influence of the war has been clear during several presidential elections, when the Vietnam War records of such candidates as Bill Clinton, George W. Bush, John Kerry, and John McCain were scrutinized by the media and the American public. Moreover, for those who fought in the war, Edidin claims, the wounds of Vietnam will never heal.

Thirty years after the last American soldier left Vietnam, the echoes of that war still reverberate in the U.S. During the 2004 presidential election, President [George W.] Bush and Senator John Kerry had to explain their actions during the war. And today many are asking whether Iraq is becoming "another Vietnam."

Is the U.S. headed for "another Vietnam" in Iraq? It's a question posed often in the media, and it's just one example of the hold that the Vietnam War still exerts on the U.S. more than 30 years after it ended.

Background to Vietnam

The longest war in American history, Vietnam divided the nation like nothing since the Civil War. More than 58,000 American soldiers died and more than 300,000 were wounded in the war, which split families, turned the old against the young, and drove a wedge of mistrust between many Americans and their leaders.

"Vietnam is still with us," according to Henry Kissinger, who was President Richard M. Nixon's Secretary of State and National Security Adviser in the late 1960s and early '70s. "It has created doubts about American judgment, about American credibility, about American power—not only at home, but throughout the world."

Unlike most wars, the war in Vietnam didn't begin with an "opening shot." Instead, the U.S. became involved gradually, beginning in 1954, when President Dwight D. Eisenhower sent military advisers to train and arm the South Vietnamese Army in its fight against Communist North Vietnam. (Vietnam had been partitioned earlier that year into North and South after the French were defeated in their effort to hold on to their century-old colonies in Indochina.)

Ho Chi Minh, the Communist and nationalist leader of the Vietminh independence movement, whose forces had defeated the French, wanted to turn all of Vietnam into a Communist state.

The Cold War

That raised alarms in Washington at a time when the Cold War between the U.S., the Soviet Union, and their allies was heating up in Asia: In 1949, Communists led by Mao Zedong had taken power in China. A year later, the Korean War began when Communist North Korea, with Soviet and Chinese support, invaded South Korea. Three years and nearly 37,000 American lives later, that war ended in a stalemate.

American officials feared that the rest of Asia could also fall. "You have a row of dominoes set up; you knock over the first one," Eisenhower said in 1954, "and what will happen to the last one is the certainty that it will go over very quickly." This "domino theory" was essentially the foundation of American policy in Vietnam for the next two decades.

When President John F. Kennedy took office in 1961, he, too, saw Vietnam as a place to demonstrate America's anti-Communist resolve. "Now we have a problem in making our power credible, and Vietnam is the place," he said in a speech that year.

By the time Kennedy was assassinated in 1963, the number of U.S. military advisers in Vietnam had risen from under 700 to roughly 16,000, and fighting between South Vietnamese and North Vietnamese troops, aided by Communist guerrillas in the South known as the Vietcong, had intensified.

In 1964, after a murky episode in which two North Vietnamese boats were said to have attacked an American destroyer in the Gulf of Tonkin off the coast of North Vietnam, President Lyndon B. Johnson asked Congress to pass the Gulf of Tonkin Resolution. It gave the President authority to "take all necessary measures to repel any armed attack against forces of the United States and to prevent further aggression."

In practice, the resolution gave the President the power to wage a war without declaring one, which would have required congressional approval.

Full-scale military intervention began in March 1965 with the arrival in Da Nang [a city in Vietnam] of the first U.S. combat troops. Johnson's war policy initially enjoyed overwhelming popular support, and by the end of the year, there were more than 200,000 U.S. troops in Vietnam—a number that would rise by the end of the decade to more than half a million.

From the start, the administration presented the conflict's progress in relentlessly optimistic terms: The war was going well and heading toward victory. As Walt Rostow, Johnson's National Security Adviser, put it in 1967: "I see the light at the end of the tunnel."

Losing a War on TV

But Vietnam was the first war in which television gave Americans regular access to relatively uncensored images of battle—G.I.s making their way through jungles and rice paddies, villagers huddled in fear outside their huts, bombs raining down from B-52 warplanes, and gory pictures of the dead and wounded of both sides. The good news from officials in Washington and U.S. commanders in Saigon seemed at odds with what people were seeing on their TVs.

"Vietnam was lost in the living rooms of America," the media scholar Marshall McLuhan wrote in 1975, "not on the battlefields of Vietnam."

As more young men were drafted to fight in a war they didn't support or understand, an antiwar movement of a sort the country had never seen began to take shape. In 1965, the first mass demonstration, with 20,000 people, took place in Washington, and the protests grew in size and militancy.

The antiwar movement dovetailed with the [African American] civil rights movement and a youth movement—sometimes called the counterculture—that emphasized experimentation and rebellion against authority. ("Don't trust anyone over 30" was a popular phrase.)

In January 1968, North Vietnam and the Vietcong launched the Tet Offensive, a series of attacks on the South during Tet, the lunar New Year. Militarily, the attack was a terrible defeat for the Communists, but grisly TV images—and just the idea that the enemy could mount such massive attacks after years of war—shook America's confidence. (It was during Tet that American troops killed hundreds of Vietnamese civilians in the village of My Lai, which became public the following year and sparked worldwide outrage.)

In March, with support for the war and his popularity plummeting, Johnson announced the start of peace talks in Paris, and declared that he would not run for a second term.

Faced with mounting turmoil over the war, Nixon, who succeeded Johnson in 1969, decided to extricate the U.S. from Vietnam. In the fall of 1969, he and Kissinger began the process of "Vietnamization": turning the fighting over to Vietnamese troops, while withdrawing U.S. forces, whose number fell to 220,000 by the end of 1970. (Nixon also widened the war in 1970 by invading Cambodia to attack Communist bases and supply lines.)

In October 1972, with U.S. troop levels in Vietnam down to about 70,000, and Nixon on his way to re-election the next month, Kissinger announced that "Peace is at hand." The Paris Peace Accords of January 1973 called for an end to the fighting and for all foreign troops to be withdrawn from Vietnam.

The Fall of Saigon

All U.S. forces came home by the end of the year, but fighting resumed in 1974. The end came in 1975: The North's forces overran the South, with Saigon falling in April, forcing the hurried evacuation of the remaining Americans and a fraction of the Vietnamese who wanted to get out.

The cost of the war to the Vietnamese was staggering, with at least 3 million people killed. More than a million fled after the war, most to the U.S., as the [Vietnamese] government sent hundreds of thousands of those left behind to "re-education [prison] camps."

After civil wars of their own, Cambodia and Laos also fell to the Communists. In Cambodia, Pol Pot [the Cambodian leader] and his Khmer Rouge [Communist Party] initiated a campaign of genocide in which up to 3 million people may have been killed.

The U.S. imposed a trade embargo on Vietnam, vast swaths of which had been destroyed by bombing and chemical defoliation. Dependent on aid from the Soviet Union, the government tried to create a Soviet-style state-run economy, which led to widespread poverty and hunger. In 1986, party leaders followed China's lead with a program of free-market economic reform, known as *doi moi*, with less state control of the economy and more private enterprise.

Since the 1990s, and especially after President Bill Clinton lifted the trade embargo in 1993, foreign investors have poured into Vietnam and the economy has boomed. But, like China, Vietnam remains a one-party Communist state, with political dissent forbidden.

Still More Questions

In the U.S., the war refuses to fade away. When he ran for President in 1992 and 1996, Clinton was hounded by accusations about not serving in Vietnam. In 2004, both candidates faced questions about their wartime actions. The Democratic nominee, Sen. John Kerry, fended off accusations that he had exaggerated his heroism as a Navy swift-boat commander in Vietnam, while President Bush denied receiving preferential treatment in joining the Texas Air National Guard as a way to stay out of Vietnam.

And the war could be a factor in the 2008 election. Sen. John McCain of Arizona, a leading contender for the Republican nomination, was a Navy pilot who spent five years as a prisoner of war in the infamous "Hanoi Hilton," where he and other P.O.W.s were tortured by their North Vietnamese captors.

The most poignant reminder of the war today may be the somber granite wall of the Vietnam Memorial in Washington, into which the names of more than 58,000 service men and women killed in the war have been inscribed.

For those who fought in Vietnam, the memorial has become a pilgrimage site; and as historian David McCullough has written, for all Americans it is a reminder of the war's cost.

"The toll in suffering, sorrow, in rancorous national turmoil can never be tabulated," he wrote. "No one wants ever to see America so divided again. And for many of the more than two million American veterans of the war, the wounds of Vietnam will never heal."

Selective Conscientious Objection to War Should Be Legalized

Gregory D. Foster

Gregory D. Foster is a professor at the National Defense University in Washington, DC, a graduate of the US Military Academy at West Point, and a decorated veteran of the Vietnam War.

Gregory D. Foster writes that although many Americans profess to be for peace as opposed to war, society glorifies soldiers who kill for the government and vilifies those men and women of conscience who refuse to partake in warfare. Currently the law does not allow for selective conscientious objection; in other words, to qualify for exempt status, a conscientious objector must be opposed to all war, philosophically or theologically, and not just to a particular conflict. This should be changed, Foster believes. In an era in which all wars are wars of choice and not necessity, the option of selective conscientious objection would protect military personnel, serve as a moral compass, and place a premium on deliberative reason instead of on religious belief. If ever there was a time when selective conscientious objection was appropriate, Foster concludes, it is now.

It is perversely ironic that we Americans, even those who profess opposition to war, generally glorify the people who fight our wars. In contrast, we usually treat conscientious objectors with undisguised disdain. They are, in the minds of many, malingerers, shirkers, cowards, even traitors, not models of principled rectitude and courage.

Not until the day comes when conscientious objectors are seen to be contributing to society rather than evading sacrifice

Gregory D. Foster, "One War at a Time: The Case for Selective Conscientious Objection," *America*, November 17, 2008. Reprinted by permission.

will they be accorded acceptance and respect. And only then will the possibility of discrediting and eliminating war as a preferred instrument of statecraft become a realizable ideal. The path to that end lies in the legitimization and institution-alization of selective conscientious objection: the currently un-accepted right of those in uniform to formally express their objection to, and refusal to serve in, particular wars.

At present, such selective opposition is proscribed [prohib-ited] by law. The legal provision covering conscientious objec-tion, found in the Military Selective Service Act, reads: "Noth-ing contained in this title . . . shall be construed to require any person to be subject to combatant training and service in the armed forces of the United States who, by reason of religious training and belief, is conscientiously opposed to participation in war in any form."

The key phrase "war in any form" is further clarified in Pentagon policy: "An individual who desires to choose the war in which he or she will participate is not a Conscientious Ob-jector under the law. The individual's objection must be to all wars rather than a specific war." Thus, an individual opposed to serving in a particular war—one badly conceived or wrong-fully conducted for instance—must, in order to be honorably discharged or assigned to noncombatant duties, demonstrate convincingly that he/she opposes all war, or be willing to face dire consequences (court-martial and possibly prison), or take more drastic action—like deserting, going absent without leave, missing troop movement or disobeying an order. For someone not opposed to all war (especially wars of necessity) and otherwise willing to serve this country in uniform, the current situation poses an intractable dilemma that argues for legalizing selective conscientious objection.

Reasons for a New Law

The need for selective objection is rooted first in the fact that the machinery of war in this country is seriously broken. All recent U.S. presidents have sought to expand and exercise their war-making powers at the expense of Congresses that consistently have favored political and ideological loyalties over their constitutional duty to check and balance executive excess. Congresses have gone to extraordinary lengths to avoid the politically risky responsibility for declaring wars and then for ending them. And the Supreme Court, abjuring its prerogative for judicial review, has resolutely refused to rule on the legality of particular wars. Thus the constitutional superstructure meant to tether the dogs of war provides precious little protection to those in uniform, the pawns of war.

The need for selective objection also rests on the contractual relationship between military personnel, the government and society. The written contract governing the men and women in uniform is their oath of office, which binds adherents to support unreservedly and defend the Constitution and obligates them to obey the lawful orders of the president and other superior officers. All in uniform therefore give dutiful, silent obedience and tacitly accept restrictions on individual rights in return for lawful, constitutional behavior by those above them in the chain of command.

But there also is a tacit social contract of mutual rights, obligations and expectations. This unwritten contract implies that in return for giving dutiful obedience and giving up certain rights, military personnel have a right to expect and receive from their superiors behavior that is not only constitutional and legal, but also ethical, competent and accountable. Where government (including the military chain of command) fails on any of these counts, the contract, and with it the reciprocal obligation for dutiful obedience and forgone rights, is broken.

Two other factors underscore the need for selective objection. Most notably, contemporary wars are no longer wars of necessity; they are, without exception, wars of choice. Yet conscientious objection is predicated on the unexamined notion that the wars we fight are wars of necessity, involving a one-way relationship of government rights and individual obligations. When wars of choice are the norm, however, when survival is not at stake and emergency conditions do not prevail, the reverse of this relationship is called for: one in which government is obligated to act responsibly and competently, while individuals in uniform retain the right not to serve (or honor their commitment) when government fails to meet its obligations.

Another factor underscoring the need for selective conscientious objection is, counterintuitively, America's volunteer military. Historically, conscientious objection has been tolerated principally because of its relationship to conscription. Some would argue that conscientious objection does not and should not apply to volunteers who have joined the military of their own volition, eyes wide open, knowing full well what to expect. Of all people, they should be willing to forsake certain rights, defer unquestioningly to higher authority and face the ultimate sacrifice.

It is instructive, however, to remind ourselves that Title 10 of the United States Code specifies the mission of the U.S. Army as not simply to wage war, but to be "capable . . . of preserving the peace and security, and providing for the defense, of the United States." Arguably, therefore, the law is on the side of those in uniform who volunteer to defend their country as a matter of necessity, not to fight wars of choice wrongly undertaken or wrongfully prosecuted.

Purposes a New Law Would Serve

Selective conscientious objection would serve three major purposes. First, it would protect military personnel by according them the most fundamental right any party to a social contract deserves: the right to withdraw from that contract (or seek redress) if the other party—the government in general, the military in particular—breaks or fails to honor it.

Second, it would serve, in the absence of conscription, as a much-needed internal moral compass for U.S. war-making. Ideally, conscription serves this purpose by creating stakeholders throughout society—especially among elites otherwise disinclined to serve or have their offspring serve—who are willing to scrutinize and restrain the use of military force. But since conscription seems destined to remain a vestige of America's past, selective objection would be a surrogate, the presumption being that legalizing the practice would embolden those in uniform—war's ultimate stakeholders—who object to wrongful and wrong-headed wars to express their opposition formally. At some point, a critical mass of such internal opposition might be reached that would force lawmakers and society to take notice and act.

Third, selective objection would place a premium on deliberative reason, rather than religious (or religious-like) belief, and thereby serve the embedded aim of producing individuals in uniform who are civically engaged and civically competent, not simply true-believing followers of religious or ideological dogma.

If ever there was a time to put a system of selective conscientious objection in place, it is now. Otherwise, individuals of conscience who are courageous enough to step outside the obedient herd will continue to attract undeserved opprobrium, war will persist as our eternal lot, and we will have only our own silent indifference to blame.

Soldiers Can Fall in Love with War

Daniel Stone

Daniel Stone has served as a senior writer for Newsweek *magazine. He has also worked on the television show* America's Most
Wanted *and has appeared as a guest on* Air America *and* CNN.

*In this viewpoint, Daniel Stone considers the lives of several Iraq
War soldiers who have signed up for multiple tours of duty because they cannot get the same satisfaction from civilian life as
they do from military service. These soldiers enjoy the thrill of
being in a combat zone, Stone writes, and often become bored
and frustrated by mundane activities back home. Despite their
love of the war zone, however, these soldiers are prone to post-
traumatic stress disorder and may struggle to maintain mar-
riages and other relationships.*

For some soldiers, there's no place like combat.

Staff Sgt. Shaun McBride would rather be in a war zone
than at home. He likes the adrenaline, he says, even the "fear
someone can shoot you." He hates the petty responsibilities of
home life, the bills and family issues.

He's clocked 43 months in Afghanistan and Iraq. His first
wife of three years sent him divorce papers while he was fighting Taliban militants—she wanted to marry a friend of his. . . .
"Whatever," says McBride, 32, with a shrug. Now he's remar-
ried—to Evangeline (Star) McBride, a 27-year-old divorced
mother of one—and getting ready for his fifth deployment
with the Third Brigade combat team of the 101st Airborne
Division.

Daniel Stone, "Love Is a Battlefield," *Newsweek*, 153-24, June 15, 2009, p. 36. Reprinted by permission.

A Soldier's Soldier

When asked in front of Star what he misses most when he's overseas, he doesn't hesitate: his souped-up Mustang. He likes to drive it fast, and "show what's what" when another flashy car pulls up next to him at a stoplight. But even the driving is better in Iraq. There, you "do whatever you want on the road. You own the road—You can go into people's houses without being invited in. It's like you own their house."

Sergeant McBride is a soldier's soldier. He knows his job, and loves it above all else. At a time when the military desperately needs trained fighting men and women, he's always ready to go. But there's also something disturbing about a young man who thrives on conflict and doesn't really feel at ease with his family. Asked the hardest part of coming home, he responds: "Having to live with other people. Having to deal." He doesn't like having to rush to pick up his stepdaughter from day care, or to get the groceries. Where is the line between the highly valued fighting man and the guy who's loving it too much, and been too long in the war zone?

A tiny fraction of Americans are doing the bulk of the country's fighting and policing in far-off lands. Less than 5 percent of Americans are in the active military at any time. Of those, a much smaller number of officers and enlisted men have done multiple tours. Most are in the Army, and less than 15 percent of Army soldiers have done three or more deployments.

Some of those men and women answer the call because they think it's their duty, whether they like it or not. Some go because it's a good way to advance their careers, or because they like the extra money they get with combat duty. Others just like it. "Soldiers want to fight," says retired Gen. Barry McCaffrey, who was the youngest and most decorated Army general when he retired in 1996. "That's why they signed up."

An Extreme Guy

First Sgt. Jason Dodge is that kind of soldier, an extreme guy
in every respect. He gets to his office between 0425 [4:25 AM]
and 0428. A few hours later, he's on his morning run—usually
10 to 15 miles. He can climb a 30-foot rope using just his
arms in 10 seconds. He works best in a room without direct
sunlight, he says, and doesn't like to eat more than one meal a
day—"and that's dinner with my wife, but only because she
makes me." His job: to engineer explosives to blow down
doors and walls.

It doesn't seem to really bother Sergeant Dodge, 36, that
most of his Army buddies have moved on, either transferring
to a nondeploying base or leaving the military altogether. He'll
miss the old tradition of going to an Outback Steakhouse
with his Army friends and their wives before and after each
deployment. . . . But the way he sees it, he's got a job to do,
and it's in Iraq or Afghanistan.

Dodge's wife, Dana, 31, says he's always himself when he
gets back from a deployment, but she does handle him carefully at first. "Maybe his temper is a bit short when he first
comes home," she says. "If he gets that look, I can just tell and
walk away for a while." She's learned not to call him and make
one request, then tack on others. She also knows he doesn't
like crowds.

Does Dodge like the war zone? "I don't look at it like that,
sir, I really don't," he says. He enjoys "playing with explosives,"
and shooting his gun, and forming the tight bonds that can
be forged in a hostile setting. But he also feels professional
satisfaction. "I haven't lost a single soldier . . . and I consider
that my biggest accomplishment," says Dodge, whose brother
died in a training accident in 1995. "If I wasn't there, I don't
know who would do my job. But what I do know is that I
would do it better."

Some soldiers enjoy the thrill of combat and sign up for multiple tours of duty when they cannot find the same satisfaction in civilian life. © Stephen Mulcahey/Alamy.

Everyone likes doing what they're good at. But soldiers have to weigh the benefits and costs in ways that others don't. The more time soldiers do in war zones, the more likely they are to suffer posttraumatic stress disorder [PTSD]. A mental-health survey conducted by the Army has quantified the psychological wear and tear of repeated tours. As of spring 2008, 27 percent of noncommissioned officers [NCOs] with three or four deployments had shown symptoms of PTSD, compared with 12 percent of those with one tour.

An optimist reading the data might point out that nearly three quarters of NCOs don't suffer any such mental-health symptoms. But in worst-case scenarios, a stressed soldier can be lethal. In early May, 44-year-old Army Sgt. John M. Russell went berserk in a military stress center in Baghdad, killing five fellow soldiers. Russell was weeks away from finishing his third tour in Iraq, and apparently thought the military was trying to get rid of him.

Over Four Years in Iraq

Army Chief Warrant Officer Robert Lakes, 39, knows that war has changed him. Everyone tells him he seems a little different after each new deployment. He looks visibly exhausted at 10 AM on a Thursday, sitting in an office with no windows at Fort Campbell, just north of Nashville. "I really got to watch it," he says. "Sometimes you get back from a normal day here [on base in the United States] and you're just blown. You just want to lay down and go to sleep. I didn't quite used to be like that. But that might just be me getting older, too. I can't really point to the war and say that did it."

After clocking an astounding 52 months in Iraq, he's planning to go again. He manages the heavy equipment that goes from Fort Campbell to Iraq, keeps it in working condition in the war zone and then ships some of it back again. That means he deploys early to prepare, and stays longer to make sure all the loose ends are tied up. "It cost me an 18-year marriage," says Lakes with an awkward laugh. "But you know, I just do what they tell me to do, go where they tell me to go. I don't think about it too much."

Lakes has a fiancee now, 38-year-old Pamela Doss. They met on Facebook, and realized they had many shared interests and traits—a love of Harley-Davidson motorcycles, a taste for marshmallows burned black. She got into the relationship knowing that he'd be deploying again and again. But she wishes it were otherwise. "I finally met someone I'm compatible with, and I have to share him with the rest of the world."

Lakes could have gotten a transfer and avoided another deployment. But like other soldiers who opt for more tours, he feels that his fellow soldiers depend on him. "There is nobody else in the unit doing my job," he says. "I don't have a choice." He hasn't seen a psychologist one-on-one, but has phoned a help center called Military OneSource to talk over divorce issues and, in one instance, stress over back-to-back deployments when he was "only home a month or so."

Holding Together a Normal Life

Many military personnel say it's not the number of tours that gets to them, but the length of each one. The Army has the longest tours, with soldiers generally doing a year or more. Army Intelligence Officer Jessica Ohle, 42, currently garrisoned at Fort Bragg in North Carolina, has logged 39 months in a combat zone (as well as additional time in the Balkans and Kuwait), and she wants to keep doing it. But she also wants shorter stints. "When I went to Bosnia in 2001, it was a seven-month deployment, and I remember thinking, this is a loooong time," she says. "But then September 11 happened, and now we're doing 12 months. Seven months now seems like a dream to me."

Part of the trouble with long tours is the stress of holding together a normal life back home. "When you're gone so long, you put your whole life on hold," says Ohle. "You can't plan anything." That can be OK if you're single, but Ohle has been dating another Army intelligence officer who is in a different brigade. They met during a training exercise many years ago, and then in 2006 spent a few months together "downrange," as Ohle calls the combat zone. After that, the dating was long distance. They've been "together-together" only since February, and Ohle expects her boyfriend to deploy again sometime this summer.

Whenever she comes back to the United States, Ohle faces culture shock similar to anyone who returns from a foreign land. She's overwhelmed by the food selection in the markets, and the number of people in the aisles. But unlike ordinary travelers, she also needs to keep her anger in check. "When someone with a shopping cart gets in your way, you can't just yell at them to get out of the way," she says. "Interacting with people requires a reset."

Post-Traumatic Stress Disorder Symptoms

Sergeant McBride and his wife know he has some PTSD-like symptoms. It's always tough when he first comes home from overseas. After his last deployment, she recalls, she suddenly dropped a laundry basket. He started screaming at her never to do that again. "He was about ready to hit the floor," she says—as if he were taking cover from an incoming round. "After three months, he gets normal again."

Star understands what bugs him about home life. "There are bills; you're getting nickeled-and-dimed all the time here," she says. "Everyday life, errands and all that." She handles the mundane duties—including the phone calls to banks or the cable-TV service. "He's kind of antisocial," she says. "It's a hassle for him." The sergeant objects: "I'm not antisocial, I just don't like dealing with strangers."

He may always have been a bit that way. McBride joined the Army in 1996, when he was just 18. That was after he'd dropped out of high school and his mother had kicked him out of the house, he says. Mom was glad when he signed up: she thought he could use the discipline. He did an early stint in Korea and had a child with his first wife. But he was back in the United States on 9/11, taking his wife for surgery that day. He dropped her at the clinic and went to breakfast at a McDonald's, where he saw the towers falling on television. He then picked up his wife, dropped her at home and said, "Sorry, I'm going to work." At the base, everyone was buzzing. "We all knew we were going to war," he says. "We were all excited about it."

Now he's in his fifth year of marriage to Star, and headed into his fifth deployment. Star knows how to handle his moods, and tries not to surprise him with much. She likes that he's an authority figure who can tell her "no," which she "missed out on growing up." When she bought a puppy during one deployment, and it chewed up a carpet, Star e-mailed a photo with a caption: "Don't kill the dog." Shaun says he was "pissed," but he's come to love the dog.

Star knows her husband is less warm than other men, those who show lots of affection to their wives. "I meet them all the time and I'm like—you exist?" she says. "He's kind of emotionally closed. Sometimes it's lonelier when he's here than when he's gone."

Letting Down His Guard

Over several interviews . . . , there were two moments when Sergeant McBride let down his tough-guy guard. The first was when he teared up recalling 9/11. The second came when he mentioned that on his upcoming tour he'd be in a desk job, orchestrating the positions of soldiers "outside the wire." To the pleasant surprise of his wife, he offered that he was "ready to take a break" from the real action.

Still, McBride insists the deployments don't wear him down psychologically. "If you want help, you can go and get help," he says. "We do suicide-prevention briefings every two months or so." But he scoffs at the suicides: "It's just a bunch of weak people." Has he ever been to a psychologist? "No. Never seen a psychologist one-on-one," he says. Star intervenes, in her usual plain-spoken manner. "He needs to. Write that down." Shaun laughs: "Whatever."

We Must Do More to Help Veterans with PTSD

Michael M. Faenza

Michael M. Faenza has served as president and CEO of the National Mental Health Association, a nonprofit organization working to improve the mental health of all Americans.

According to Michael M. Faenza, post-traumatic stress disorder (PTSD) has long been misunderstood, and even today, proper treatment is hampered by a number of factors. PTSD is an often debilitating condition that can occur after a traumatic event. It can manifest itself in the form of nightmares, flashbacks, anxiety, depression, and other symptoms. Many soldiers are reluctant to admit that they suffer from psychological trauma, Faenza explains, and accurate diagnosis is often difficult. With well over a hundred thousand soldiers fighting in Iraq, and as many as 30 percent suffering from some form of PTSD, Faenza maintains that there is much work left to do to ensure that these soldiers make a healthy and productive return to society.

It is hard to believe, but fewer than a hundred years ago, European combat soldiers who developed tremors and nightmares were executed as traitors or branded as weaklings.

Thankfully, we have made significant progress since then. We now know that it is normal for servicemembers to develop traumatic reactions when they return from war. We are no longer surprised that some experience difficulty adjusting back in their communities and may even experience mental health problems. We are not shocked that, as a result, divorce rates for returning soldiers have skyrocketed. And we cannot

Michael M. Faenza, "The War at Home: Addressing PTSD Among Returning Servicemembers," *The Officer*, 81-9, 2005. Reprinted by permission.

escape headlines about combat veterans involved in acts of violence and even tragic instances of suicide after experiencing the hardship of war.

The Prevalence of PTSD

Yet, despite our greater understanding, our nation still has a long way to go in recognizing the mental health needs of our returning heroes. Furthermore, our military engagement in Iraq and Afghanistan, with its heavy reliance on Reserve and [National] Guard forces, and extended deployments and re-deployments, present uncharted territory for soldiers' mental health.

Currently [in 2005], there are 140,000 troops in Iraq alone; 40 percent are either Reservists or National Guard troops. And many of these individuals must stay on well beyond their discharge date—sometimes for an additional 18 months. These hard-working soldiers are not full-time military personnel and have not received the level of training and preparation necessary to manage these circumstances. Armed conflict, death of unit members, threat of capture, long stretches away from home, extreme physical conditions and other circumstances all wear on these troops—ultimately putting them at risk of post-traumatic stress disorder (PTSD) and other mental health problems, such as depression, anxiety or substance abuse.

The statistics are compelling: more than 30 percent of soldiers returning from Iraq report mental health problems, according to government studies. Anxiety, depression, nightmares, anger and inability to concentrate: these problems emerge immediately after soldiers leave the theater. But more serious and dangerous problems often lay dormant, surfacing months—if not years—later, with potentially long-term consequences.

While a servicemember may escape physical injury and appear to return home "safely," he or she remains at high risk of adjustment problems and, in many cases, PTSD, an often debilitating condition that can occur after exposure to a terrifying event, especially when grave physical harm occurred or was threatened. PTSD is often diagnosed when an individual experiences emotional numbness and sleep disturbances, depression, anxiety, irritability or angry outbursts and feelings of guilt for a month or more. While symptoms typically begin within three months of a traumatic event, they can take years to develop. And, the severity and duration of PTSD varies; some people recover within six months, others may experience problems indefinitely.

Many people with PTSD repeatedly re-experience the trauma in the form of flashbacks, memories, nightmares or frightening thoughts, especially when facing events or objects reminiscent of the event. Anniversaries of the ordeal can also trigger symptoms.

Lately, we have heard primarily of acute PTSD in first-responders, such as emergency medical technicians, police and firefighters and even media professionals covering tragic events. The 9/11 terrorist attacks gave the disorder greater visibility, and the devastating effects of Hurricane Katrina will continue to have an emotional impact on the victims and first-responders for years to come.

Problems in Diagnosing and Treating PTSD

Unfortunately, it is too early to assess the big picture, to know how many returning troops may suffer from PTSD. For example, in a study of Gulf War veterans, the prevalence of PTSD more than doubled between the initial assessment and a follow-up assessment two years later. We also know that many veterans who appear to have combat-related mental health problems often avoid seeking medical care despite high success rates, due principally to stigma associated with these disorders. In fact, a recent Department of Defense Study showed that six of 10 who showed signs of mental-health problems believed their commanders would treat them differently and that fellow troops would lose confidence in them if they sought care; fewer than half sought help. Clearly, shame, fear of repercussions and denial of mental-health problems are formidable obstacles for servicemembers.

Furthermore, many medical providers miss opportunities to diagnose PTSD because it commonly occurs simultaneously with other health problems. Sufferers may experience substance abuse problems, headaches, gastrointestinal complaints, immune system problems, dizziness, chest pain or discomfort in other parts of the body. Doctors often treat these symptoms without knowing that they stem from PTSD.

The impact of war is far greater than just on the individual soldier, as well. The psychological stress of a soldier's return—especially a soldier suffering with PTSD—can take a toll on family members, who often live in fear for the well-being of their loved ones, face readjustment issues after prolonged separation, and must handle the uncertainty associated with future deployment, extended tours of duty and other stresses of an overextended military.

Luckily, servicemembers can recover from PTSD. Research demonstrates the effectiveness of cognitive-behavioral therapy, group therapy and exposure therapy (in which an individual repeatedly relives the traumatic experience under controlled conditions to work through the trauma). Medications can help ease symptoms of depression and anxiety, and help promote sleep. Scientists continue to research which treatments work best for which type of trauma. But we do know that early intervention is important in helping avoid long-term symptoms.

The bottom line: War produces psychiatric casualties just as it does other kinds of casualties. Our society must commit to a comprehensive response to help support the recovery of our troops.

New Initiatives in Treating PTSD

The National Mental Health Association (NMHA) believes it is its responsibility, and great honor, to offer assistance to servicemembers and their families. The public has flooded NMHA with requests for this type of support dating back to the Gulf War, with a substantial spike after the 9/11 terrorist attacks. . . .

The overwhelming response to NMHA's outreach has uncovered a need for much more. So, in a first-of-its-kind collaboration among military organizations, corporations and the community at large, NMHA launched Operation Healthy Reunions, a program to support the mental health of troops returning from Iraq and Afghanistan, veterans of past wars, and soldiers traumatized by Hurricane Katrina relief work, terrorist attacks and other events requiring them to bravely serve the country. NMHA's goal is to ensure that servicemembers receive the information, support and services they need and deserve.

Specifically, Operation Healthy Reunions provides education and helps to break down the stigma surrounding mental health problems among soldiers, their families and medical staff: Through a variety of distribution channels, NMHA provides materials on such topics as reuniting with your spouse and children, adjusting after war, depression and PTSD.

Not surprisingly, the reception to Operation Healthy Reunions has been exceedingly positive. In fact, CPT [Captain] Vanessa White, a clinical social worker serving on a Combat Stress Control team near An Najaf, Iraq, recently wrote to NMHA and said:

> The stress of living in a combat zone for months on end can be overwhelming. Separation from loved ones; facing death and the uncertainty of war; living in austere conditions; and dealing with divorce, infidelity, and financial problems—all while 7,000 miles away from home—can really take a toll.

We are thrilled to hear about Operation Healthy Reunions, which will greatly fill the void when we return. Thanks!

Captain White's message is a poignant reminder that we have much left to do to guarantee that the men and women we employ overseas return safely and have the support and services needed for happy, healthy, productive lives at home.

For Further Discussion

1. How did Tim O'Brien's Vietnam War experiences play a role in his subsequent writing career? (*See* Lee, Hicks.)

2. Many critics characterize O'Brien as a Vietnam War writer. What elements of his writing force readers to think of him as more than just a war novelist? (*See* Lee.)

3. From his writings, it is clear that O'Brien views the Vietnam War as a mistake. Is war a necessary evil, or can it be avoided by diplomacy and other means? (*See* O'Brien, Bresler, Pilger.)

4. O'Brien stresses the notion of how to tell a "true" war story. What, according to O'Brien, makes a war story a true one? (*See* Harris, Kaplan, Ringnalda, Calloway, Bates.)

5. Does the ending of *The Things They Carried* conclude the book satisfactorily, or does it purposefully leave the story unresolved? (*See* Bates, Blyn.)

6. Which details in the text of *The Things They Carried* lead the reader to believe that the story is nonfiction? Which details suggest that it is fiction? Why does O'Brien mix the two genres so liberally? (*See* Harris, Kaplan, Ringnalda, Calloway, Bates.)

7. What are some of the struggles that returning war veterans must deal with? How are various organizations attempting to help them? (*See* Edidin, Stone, Faenza.)

8. Why are some soldiers more comfortable during war than in peacetime? (*See* Stone.)

For Further Reading

Stephen Crane, *The Red Badge of Courage*. New York: D. Appleton, 1895.

Joseph Heller, *Catch-22*. New York: Simon and Schuster, 1961.

Ernest Hemingway, *A Farewell to Arms*. New York: Charles Scribner's Sons, 1929.

————, *For Whom the Bell Tolls*. New York: Charles Scribner's Sons, 1940.

————, *The Sun Also Rises*. New York: Charles Scribner's Sons, 1926.

Michael Herr, *Dispatches*. New York: Knopf, 1977.

Homer, *The Iliad*. Various editions.

Norman Mailer, *The Naked and the Dead*. New York: Holt, Rinehart and Winston, 1948.

Tim O'Brien, *Going After Cacciato*. New York: Delacorte/ Seymour Lawrence, 1978.

————, *If I Die in a Combat Zone, Box Me Up and Ship Me Home*. New York: Delacorte, 1973.

————, *In the Lake of the Woods*. Boston: Houghton Mifflin/ Seymour Lawrence, 1994.

————, *Northern Lights*. New York: Delacorte/Seymour Lawrence, 1975.

Erich Maria Remarque, *All Quiet on the Western Front*. Boston: Little, Brown, 1929.

Dalton Trumbo, *Johnny Got His Gun*. New York: Lippincott, 1939.

Kurt Vonnegut, *Slaughterhouse-Five* New York: Delacorte, 1969.

Walt Whitman, *Specimen Days*, in *Complete Prose Works*. Philadelphia: David McKay, 1892.

Bibliography

Books

Philip D. Beidler *Late Thoughts on an Old War: The Legacy of Vietnam.* Athens: University of Georgia Press, 2004.

Philip D. Beidler *Re-writing America: Vietnam Authors in Their Generation.* Athens: University of Georgia Press, 1991.

David Bevan *Literature and War.* Amsterdam: Rodopi, 1990.

Brenda M. Boyle *Masculinity in Vietnam War Narratives: A Critical Study of Fiction, Films and Nonfiction Writings.* Jefferson, NC: McFarland, 2009.

Kenton J. Clymer *The Vietnam War: Its History, Literature and Music.* El Paso: Texas Western Press, 1998.

Christopher Donovan *Postmodern Counternarratives: Irony and Audience in the Novels of Paul Auster, Don DeLillo, Charles Johnson, and Tim O'Brien.* New York: Routledge, 2005.

Paul Fussell *The Great War and Modern Memory.* New York: Oxford University Press, 1975.

Barry Gilmore and Alexander Kaplan	*Tim O'Brien in the Classroom: "This Too Is True: Stories Can Save Us".* Urbana, IL: National Council of Teachers of English, 2007.
Mark A. Heberle	*Thirty Years After: New Essays on Vietnam War Literature, Film, and Art.* Newcastle upon Tyne, UK: Cambridge Scholars, 2009.
Tobey C. Herzog	*Writing Vietnam, Writing Life: Caputo, Heinemann, O'Brien, Butler.* Iowa City: University of Iowa Press, 2008.
Walter L. Hixson	*Historical Memory and Representations of the Vietnam War.* New York: Garland, 2000.
A.D. Horne	*The Wounded Generation: America After Vietnam.* Englewood Cliffs, NJ: Prentice-Hall, 1981.
Philip K. Jason	*Acts and Shadows: The Vietnam War in American Literary Culture.* Lanham, MD: Rowman & Littlefield, 2000.
Steven Kaplan	*Understanding Tim O'Brien.* Columbia: University of South Carolina Press, 1995.
Catherine Mary McLoughlin	*The Cambridge Companion to War Writing.* New York: Cambridge University Press, 2009.
Thomas Myers	*Walking Point: American Narratives of Vietnam.* New York: Oxford University Press, 1988.

Margot Norris   *Writing War in the Twentieth Century.* Charlottesville: University Press of Virginia, 2000.

Stewart O'Nan   *The Vietnam Reader: The Definitive Collection of American Fiction and Nonfiction on the War.* New York: Anchor Books, 1998.

Angela K. Smith   *Gender and Warfare in the Twentieth Century: Textual Representations.* Manchester, UK: Manchester University Press, 2004.

Patrick A. Smith   *Tim O'Brien: A Critical Companion.* Westport, CT: Greenwood, 2005.

James Tatum   *The Mourner's Song: War and Remembrance from "The Iliad" to Vietnam.* Chicago: University of Chicago Press, 2003.

Alex Vernon and Catherine Calloway   *Approaches to Teaching the Works of Tim O'Brien.* New York: Modern Language Association of America, 2010.

Jeffrey Walsh   *American War Literature, 1914 to Vietnam.* New York: St. Martin's, 1982.

Andrew A. Wiest, Mary Barbier, and Glenn Robins   *America and the Vietnam War: Re-examining the Culture and History of a Generation.* New York: Routledge, 2010.

Periodicals

Maria S. Bonn	"Can Stories Save Us? Tim O'Brien and the Efficacy of the Text," *Critique*, Fall 1994.
Christopher D. Campbell	"Conversation Across a Century: The War Stories of Ambrose Bierce and Tim O'Brien," *War, Literature, and the Arts*, Fall/Winter 1998.
Tina Chen	"Unraveling the Deeper Meaning: Exile and the Embodied Poetics of Displacement in Tim O'Brien's *The Things They Carried*," *Contemporary Literature*, vol. 39, no. 1, 1998.
Renée Epstein	"Talking Dirty: Memories of War and the Vietnam Novel," *Massachusetts Review*, vol. 34, no. 3, 1993.
Edward Hagan and John Briggs	"Tim O'Brien's Ironic Aesthetic: What Is the Nature of a 'True' Story?," *Recorder: Journal of the American Irish Historical Society*, vol. 16, no. 2, 2003.
Herbert Hendin and Ann Pollinger Haas	"Suicide and Guilt as Manifestations of PTSD in Vietnam Combat Veterans," *American Journal of Psychiatry*, vol. 148, 1991.
Carl S. Horner	"Challenging the Law of Courage and Heroic Identification in Tim O'Brien's *If I Die in a Combat Zone* and *The Things They Carried*," *War, Literature, and the Arts*, vol. 11, no. 1, 1999.

David R. Jarraway — "'Excremental Assault' in Tim O'Brien: Trauma and Recovery in Vietnam War Literature," *Modern Fiction Studies*, vol. 44, no. 3, Fall 1998.

Philip K. Jason — "The Noise Is Always in My Head: Auditory Images in the Vietnam War," *Midwest Quarterly*, vol. 37, no. 3, 1996.

Steven Kaplan — "The Undying Uncertainty of the Narrator in Tim O'Brien's 'The Things They Carried,'" *Critique*, Fall 1993.

T.J. Lustig — "'Moments of Punctuation': Metonymy and Ellipsis in Tim O'Brien," *Yearbook of English Studies*, vol. 31, 2001.

Daniel Robinson — "Getting It Right: The Short Fiction of Tim O'Brien," *Critique*, Spring 1999.

Lorrie N. Smith — "The Things Men Do: The Gendered Subtext in Tim O'Brien's *Esquire* Stories," *Critique*, Fall 1994.

Mark Taylor — "Tim O'Brien's War," *Centennial Review*, vol. 39, no. 2, 1995.

John H. Timmerman — "Tim O'Brien and the Art of the True War Story: 'Night March' and 'Speaking of Courage,'" *Twentieth Century Literature*, Spring 2000.

Daniel L. Zins   "Imagining the Real: The Fiction of Tim O'Brien," *Hollins Critic*, June 1986.

Index

CPSIA information can be obtained
at www.ICGtesting.com
Printed in the USA
FFOW021030290413
1141FF

9 780737 754605